Why Organic Farming is Great for Canada

By

Leroy A. Brown

© 2013 Leroy A. Brown

ISBN 978-0-9936618-0-8

Published by

Cariporter Inc

465 Yonge St PO Box 73021 Wood St PO,

Toronto, ON M4Y 2W5, Canada

Email: cariporterltd@gmail.com

Website: www.cariporter.ca

RIGHTS

All rights reserved. No part of this publication is to be reproduced or used in any manner whatsoever, without written permission from the publisher.

LIABILITY

The publisher and the author make no representations, guarantees or warranties.

Some materials in this publication are not specific to organic agriculture, but they can be applied to it.

TRADEMARK

All trademarks, trade names, logos, etc., used or mentioned in this book are the property of their respective owners.

CARIPORTER

FOR ORGANIC CONSULTATION, ORGANIC BOOKS, ORGANIC FOOD, ETC.

Website: www.cariporter.ca

Email: cariporterltd@gmail.com

Facebook: facebook.com/cariporter

Twitter: @cariporter1

Yes Organic

FOR FUN ABOUT ORGANIC, SOCIAL NETWORK, ETC.

Website: www.yesorganic.ca

Email: yesorganic17@gmail.com

Facebook: facebook.com/yesorganic

Twitter: @yesorganic1

TABLE OF CONTENTS

7	**About the Author**	
8	**Acknowledgements**	
10	**Introduction**	
11		Global
12		North America
14		Canada
18	**Organic World**	
18		What is organic?
20		Governance
20	....	*Organic Products Regulations (OPR)*
20	....	*Canadian Organic Standards (COS)*
20	....	*Canada Organic Logo*
20	....	*Canada Organic Office Operating Manual 2008*
20	....	*Canadian Food Inspection Agency (CFIA)*
21	....	*Accredited Certification Bodies*
21	....	*Food and Agriculture Regulations and Acts*
21		Movement
22	....	*Canadian Organic Growers (COG)*
23	....	*International Federation of Organic Agriculture Movements (IFOAM)*
24		International Organic Sector

26	**Agriculture Canada**	
26	………………………..	*Agriculture and Agri-Food Canada (AAFC)*
26	………………………..	*Vision*
26	………………………..	*Agriculture Policy Framework*
26	………………………..	*Growing Forward*
27	………………………..	*Partners and Agencies*
30	Agricultural Statistics	
37	Canadian Organic Sector	
42	**So Why is Organic Farming Great for Canada?**	
42	The Obvious	
44	The Environment	
45	Domestic and International Markets	
46	Tourism	
47	Health	
48	Farm Operation	
50	**Examples of Enterprises that Sell Organic Food**	
50	………………………..	*Blacks Family Farm in Manitoba*
51	………………………..	*Choices Markets in British Columbia*
52	………………………..	*Ferme Alva Farm in New Brunswick*
53	**What is the Difference between Natural and Organic?**	
54	**Innovations and Happenings in Canada**	
60	………………………..	*Agricultural Awards*
65	………………………..	*Immigration*

66	**Investments in Organic Agriculture in Canada**	
68	**Genetically Modified Organisms (GMOs)**	
68	....	*What is genetic modification (GM)?*
68	....	*So what is a genetically modified organism (GMO)?*
68	....	*Evidence–based examination of GMOs*
69	....	*Examples of Countries that have banned GMOs in one way or another*
70	....	*Examples of Countries and Regions that approve, grow and/or produce GMOs*
71	**My Thoughts**	
74	**Appendix A**	A Simple Guide to Starting an Organic Farm Operation
76	**Appendix B**	A Simple Guide to Growing Organic Crops
78	**Appendix C**	A Simple Guide to Rearing Organic Animals
80	**Appendix D**	Example of Farm Layout
81	**Appendix E**	Components of a Simple Business Plan
82	**Appendix F**	Examples of Organizations in Canada Related to Organic and/or Sustainable Agriculture
86	**Appendix G**	Examples of Institutions that Offer Organic, Sustainable and General Agriculture Education
89	**Appendix H**	Organic Careers
90	**Glossary**	
92	**Works Cited**	
94	**Index**	

ABOUT THE AUTHOR

Mr. Leroy A. Brown is an Organic Farming Consultant specializing in project and overall farm management, farm and business plans development, converting to organic and getting certified, marketing, sales, research, grant and proposal writing, and international trade.

Additionally, he has been consulted on growing warm crops in cold climates; roof top and urban gardening; determining suitability of land for organic farming; growing crops; rearing animals; and setting up a farm business among other things.

He has assisted farm operations across Canada; participated in creating and managing urban gardens in the Greater Toronto Area (GTA); and farmed in various provinces.

Mr. Brown is a member of several farm and environmental organizations nationally and internationally.

Mr. Brown has been involved in organic agriculture from farming and attending workshops, to participating in drafting standards and policy.

In addition to his years of involvement in gardening and farming, he has developed skills, knowledge and experience in other areas such as logistics, business, recycling and waste management.

He is a dedicated supporter of farming and environmental causes, both professionally and voluntarily.

ACKNOWLEDGEMENTS

I would like to thank **Andrea Douglas B.Sc., Cert CII** from Jamaica and the Cayman Islands for her review and ideas for this research. Also, her professional career in the financial and insurance sector was helpful in exploring the economic benefits of organic farming.

Thank you to **Karen Hinds and her husband Collin** in Canada for their continuous support.

Thank you to **Mr. Leroy Brown** from the United States of America (USA) for his overall support.

Thank you to **Tameca Brown** from Ecuador for sharing her international experience.

Thank you to **Stephane Ippersiel**, Manager – Video and Exhibit Services at Agriculture and Agri-Food Canada for assistance in ensuring information was updated.

Thank you to **Paul and his wife Karen** who operate a dairy farm in Ontario for taking the time to transport me across the country, and sharing their knowledge about farming in Canada.

Thank you to **Ammanie and her husband Richard, Empress, Blake, Orrette and his wife Sandra,** and **Ashley Smith** in Canada for their support.

Also, I would like to thank **Hariette, Ofeseygo, Orville, Aldane and his wife Naticha** in Jamaica for their continued support.

Thank you to **Bayley Boles** from Manitoba for being so nice, and keeping up with my never-ending talk about organic farming.

Thank you to **Jamie Reaume**, Executive Director of Holland Marsh Growers' Association, and **Jason R. Verkaik**, owner of Carron Farms in Ontario, for adjusting their schedules in order to facilitate my tour of the most concentrated area of vegetable production in Canada – Holland Marsh.

Thank you **Shawn Janse**, Research Manager at the Muck Crop Research Station in Canada, for aiding in my further understanding of the scientific analysis of crops and soils.

Also, thank you to **Dr. Kerrett Wallace**, medical doctor at the University of Manitoba, for taking time out of his busy schedule to give me a tour of Manitoba.

And thank you to all who have contributed.

Leroy A. Brown

Urban organic farming by members of Cultivate Toronto courtesy of Leroy A. Brown

INTRODUCTION

Organic agriculture is no longer a small sector, it is **big business**. There are still many small-scale farmers, but there are a growing number of larger farm operations. Organic food has expanded from farmers' markets, health food and specialty stores, to mainstream retail outlets like supermarkets and e-commerce sites. Organic farming as a sector has grown consistently in Canada and globally. Overall, the growth has been as low as four percent (4%), to as high as twenty percent (20%) annually. Per organic operation, growth has exceeded over fifty percent (50%) in some cases.

This phenomenon is largely a result of consumers' attitudes towards wanting to know where their food is coming from, and wanting to live healthier and environmentally friendly lives.

This change in behaviour is not endemic to Canada, but is happening globally, and has started a worldwide movement.

This exploration is intended to provide useful information and analyses about organic farming in Canada and internationally. Organic agriculture has the potential to be a very "**strong sustainable economic sector**, where among others, the following can be achieved:

- Increase in the standard of living;
- Increase in earnings;
- And ecological protection and conservation."[1]

Organic farming is one of the few economic activities on a growing scale (if not the only one) that protects and improves the environment, while contributing significantly to a country's overall industrial prospects.

---

[1] Leroy Brown. (2012). Why Organic Farming is Great for Jamaica.

11 GLOBAL

Across the globe, "...sales of organic food and drink reached 59 billion US dollars in 2010 according to Organic Monitor. The market has expanded over three-fold in ten years (2000: 17.9 billion US dollars). The countries with the largest markets were the United States, Germany and France, and the highest per capita consumption was in Switzerland, Denmark and Luxemburg."[2]

The sizes of various markets were as follows:

United States of America (USA)	US$26.7 billion[3]
Germany	US$8.4 billion[4]
France	US$4.7 billion[5]

"The per capita consumptions were as follows:"[6]

Switzerland	US$213[7]
Denmark	US$198[8]
Luxemburg	US$177[9]

---

[2] Research Institute of Organic Agriculture (FiBL) and International Federation of Organic Agriculture Movements (IFOAM). (2012). The World of Organic Agriculture, Statistics and Emerging Trends 2012. Rheinbreitbach, Germany: Medienhaus Plump.

[3] Research Institute of Organic Agriculture (FiBL) and International Federation of Organic Agriculture Movements (IFOAM). (2012). The World of Organic Agriculture, Statistics and Emerging Trends 2012. Rheinbreitbach, Germany: Medienhaus Plump.

[4] Research Institute of Organic Agriculture (FiBL) and International Federation of Organic Agriculture Movements (IFOAM). (2012). The World of Organic Agriculture, Statistics and Emerging Trends 2012. Rheinbreitbach, Germany: Medienhaus Plump.

[5] Research Institute of Organic Agriculture (FiBL) and International Federation of Organic Agriculture Movements (IFOAM). (2012). The World of Organic Agriculture, Statistics and Emerging Trends 2012. Rheinbreitbach, Germany: Medienhaus Plump.

[6] Leroy Brown. (2012). Why Organic Farming is Great for Jamaica.

[7] Research Institute of Organic Agriculture (FiBL) and International Federation of Organic Agriculture Movements (IFOAM). (2012). The World of Organic Agriculture, Statistics and Emerging Trends 2012. Rheinbreitbach, Germany: Medienhaus Plump.

[8] Research Institute of Organic Agriculture (FiBL) and International Federation of Organic Agriculture Movements (IFOAM). (2012). The World of Organic Agriculture, Statistics and Emerging Trends 2012. Rheinbreitbach, Germany: Medienhaus Plump.

12 NORTH AMERICA

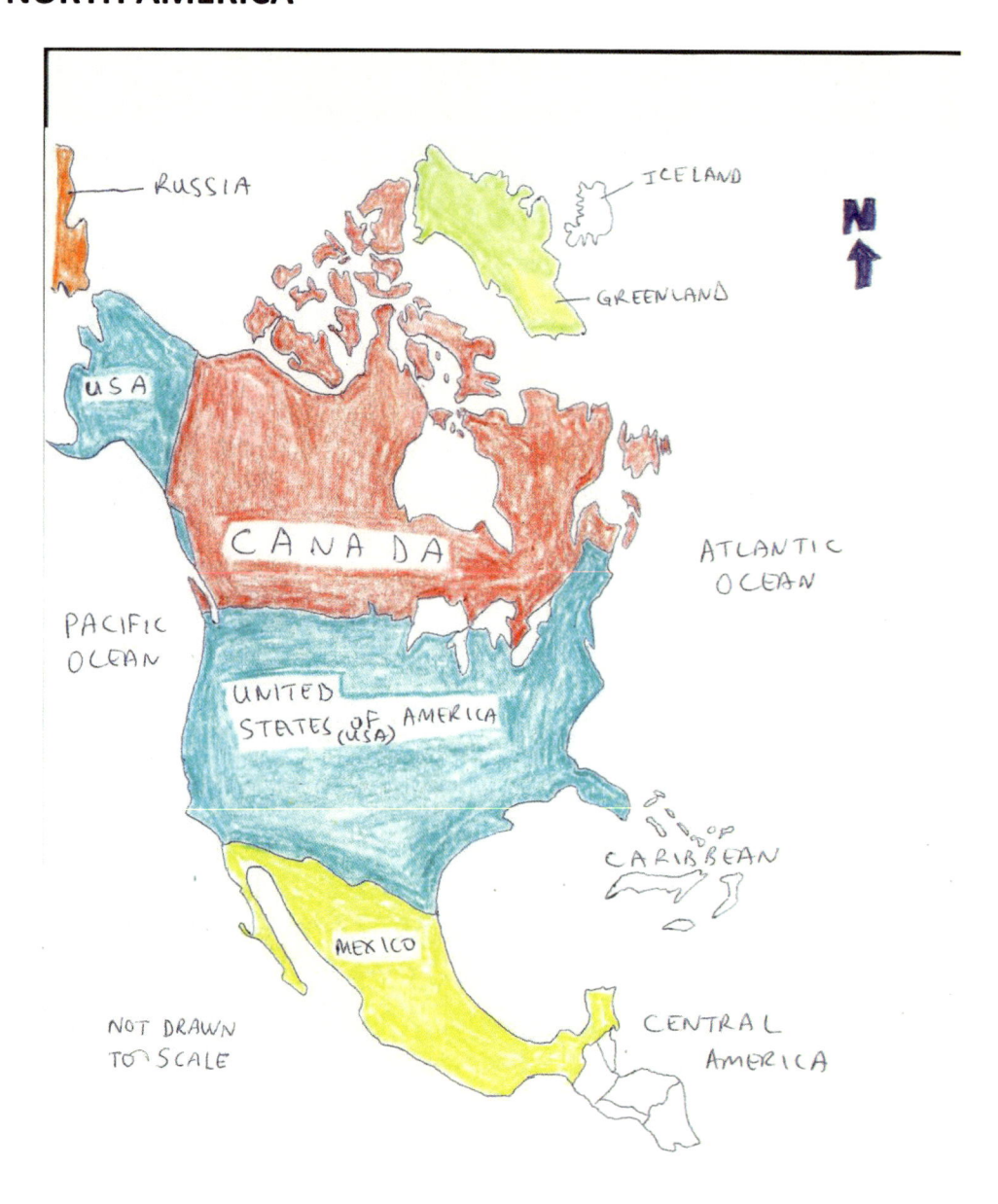

Map of North America courtesy of Leroy A. Brown

---

[9] Research Institute of Organic Agriculture (FiBL) and International Federation of Organic Agriculture Movements (IFOAM). (2012). The World of Organic Agriculture, Statistics and Emerging Trends 2012. Rheinbreitbach, Germany: Medienhaus Plump.

North America is a continent with a huge land mass. It is surrounded by fantastic geological areas such as the Arctic Ocean in the north, the Atlantic Ocean in the east, the Pacific Ocean in the west and south, and the Caribbean Sea and Mexico in the southeast.

It is the third largest continent in terms of area, after Asia and Africa.

North America has a lot of plains, high lands, deserts, forests, frigid areas and so on. There are prominent cities and cultural features such as the Theatre District in New York (in the United States of America), and the Scotiabank Caribbean Carnival in Toronto (in Canada).

Scotiabank Caribbean Carnival courtesy of Leroy A. Brown

As part of its structure, North America has rock formations that were created over many years. One of these formations is the Canadian Shield.

Canadian Shield courtesy of The Canadian Shield Foundation

CANADA

Canada is in the northern most part of North America. It is the second largest country in the world in terms of area, and shares the world's longest border with the United States of America (USA).

The land that is now Canada was first inhabited by the Inuit and First Nations people. Thereafter came the Europeans, primarily the French and the British.

The War of 1812 saw Great Britain, its colonies and Indians join forces to stop the northern expansion of the United States (US). The last battle of The War of 1812 was fought on June 30, 1815, in the Indian Ocean between the USS Peacock and the East India naval vessel, Nautilus.

In 1867, *The Constitution Act* was created, and from here on provinces decided to become federally united and self-governed. However, ties with the Queen of England were maintained.

In 1982, *The Canada Act* was passed, that gave Canada greater autonomy from Britain.

Leroy A. Brown   Why Organic Farming is Great for Canada

Canada's capital is Ottawa, and Canada has a population of over 35 million people. It is known largely for its natural resources such as oil, lumber and potash. There are other important economic activities such as hydroelectric power and telecommunications.

Additionally, Canada is becoming more globally known as follows: a major exporter and importer of agricultural goods; a nation with advances in technology such as the early success of BlackBerry; a creative country such as its world-renowned Cirque du Soleil organization, which is known for its dramatic performances and circus events; a jurisdiction with a strong financial system as was demonstrated during the recession, where Canada was one of the few countries that did not have to do a lot to keep its banks operational and solvent; and it is home to the world's leading gold producer – Barrick Gold.

Environmentally, Canada has the world's most known environmental non-government organization – Greenpeace.

Canada is a developed country with a multicultural population, and it is a member of various organizations such as the World Trade Organization (WTO), Commonwealth and G7 just to name a few.

Agri-Food Sector

The agri–food sector is a great area to invest in Canada. It is very dynamic. There is an abundance of raw materials, large masses of land for farming, skilled personnel are available, and in peak times, additional labour can be had through the temporary workers program. Also, Canada has access to global markets such as the US, the Caribbean, Europe, South Korea, India and China.

There are two (2) opportunities in the agri–food sector that are purported to have and will continue to have great potential, which are functional foods and food and beverage manufacturing. These are simply various ways in which one can create value-added products in the food chain.

Map of Canada courtesy of Maps of World.com

Functional foods are basically foods that have additional ingredients that are there to do a specific job, such as preventing individuals from chronic diseases. For example, lycopene may be added to ketchup to help prevent prostate cancer.

Food and beverage manufacturing is basically making raw materials into food, and/or food into other types of food. For example, wheat (raw material) is made into wheat flour, which is then used to make bread (food); and apples (food) are made into apple pie (other type of food).

Leroy A. Brown

Why Organic Farming is Great for Canada

Apple pie courtesy of Leroy A. Brown

"The food and beverage processing industry is the largest manufacturing industry in Canada in terms of value of production with shipments worth $92.9 billion; it accounts for 16% of total manufacturing shipments and for 2% of the national Gross Domestic Product (GDP). It's the largest manufacturing employer ..."[10] It employs about 290,000[11] persons.

---

[10] "Significance of the Food and Beverage Processing Industry in Canada." Agriculture and Agri-Food Canada, *Agr.gc.ca*. http://www.agr.gc.ca/eng/industry-markets-and-trade/statistics-and-market-information/by-product-sector/processed-food-and-beverages/significance-of-the-food-and-beverage-processing-industry-in-canada/?id=1174563085690

[11] "Significance of the Food and Beverage Processing Industry in Canada." Agriculture and Agri-Food Canada, *Agr.gc.ca*. http://www.agr.gc.ca/eng/industry-markets-and-trade/statistics-and-market-information/by-product-sector/processed-food-and-beverages/significance-of-the-food-and-beverage-processing-industry-in-canada/?id=1174563085690

ORGANIC WORLD

WHAT IS ORGANIC?

Organic is a process within which crops are grown, animals are reared, food and beverages are manufactured using non-conventional methods, such as not using synthesized herbicides and pesticides for weeds and crops; not using genetically modified (GM) seeds; and not using growth hormones in animals, just to highlight a few. It involves the use of compost and worm castings as fertilizers; it is planting legumes to help return nutrients back to the soil; it is crop rotating and intercropping; it is growing animals like cows on grass, organic alfalfa and organic grain as food, and allowing them to grow and develop as nature intended for them, and so on.

Therefore, organic farming is doing agriculture in such a way that it protects the environment, and makes humans, plants and animals healthier.

In order to let the general public know that a food product is indeed organic, if word of mouth and/or touring the farm/food operation is not sufficient, the producer will have his/her establishment assessed by an authorized certifier, before organic designation is given. This certification allows the farmer to sell not just locally, but nationally and globally.

Organic farming is more about wholesomeness rather than financial gains. And if done properly, it will result in a lot of money being earned, like what is being experienced by many of the stakeholders (such as farmers, distributors and retailers). However, if the aim is solely to make money, and to do so at any cost like in many large conventional food operations, then there will be far more losses than gains.

The Canadian Organic Growers (COG) goes on to define organic as "… the only type of agriculture with a set of principles that puts nature first. These principles are enshrined in industry-developed standards approved by consumers and verified annually by third-party organizations. As of 2009, federal organic standards are now backed by government regulation and oversight.

Organic standards are based on seven general principles:

1. Protect the environment, minimize soil degradation and erosion, decrease pollution, optimize biological productivity and promote a sound state of health.

2. Maintain long-term soil fertility by optimizing conditions for biological activity within the soil.

3. Maintain biological diversity within the system.

4. Recycle materials and resources to the greatest extent possible within the enterprise.

5. Provide attentive care that promotes the health and meets the behavioural needs of livestock.

6. Prepare organic products, emphasizing careful processing, and handling methods in order to maintain the organic integrity and vital qualities of the products at all stages of production.

7. Rely on renewable resources in locally organized agricultural systems."[12]

Internationally, organic can be defined as "… a production system that sustains the health of soils, ecosystems and people. It relies on ecological processes, biodiversity and cycles adapted to local conditions, rather than the use of inputs with adverse effects. Organic agriculture combines tradition, innovation and science to benefit the shared environment and promote fair relationships and a good quality of life for all involved."[13]

"According to the International Federation of Organic Agriculture Movements (IFOAM), organic agriculture is based on the following:

~ The principle of health;

~ The principle of ecology;

~ The principle of fairness;

~ And the principle of care."[14]

---

[12] "What is Organic?" Canadian Organic Growers, *Cog.ca*. http://www.cog.ca/about_organics/what_is_organics/

[13] Leroy Brown. (2012). Why Organic Farming is Great for Jamaica.

[14] Leroy Brown. (2012). Why Organic Farming is Great for Jamaica.

GOVERNANCE

Organic agriculture is overseen by the respective governments under which farm operators function. These governments have policies in place and organic standards that must be followed in order to be certified organic. These governments normally have agencies or bodies that regulate and certify food operations.

"On June 30, 2009, the **Organic Products Regulations (OPR)** came into effect, making the **Canadian Organic Standards (COS)** mandatory. The OPR will legally require organic products to be certified according to the COS if they are traded across provincial or international borders or use the **Canada Organic Logo**."[15]

The **Canada Organic Office Operating Manual 2008** details the administration and enforcement of the OPR.

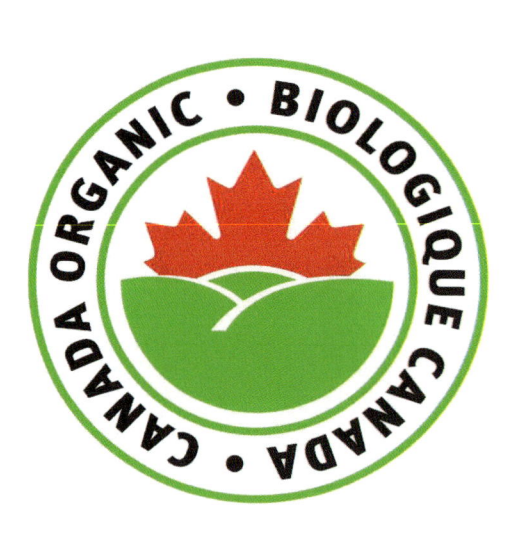

Canadian Organic Logo courtesy of the Canada Organic Office

The **Canadian Food Inspection Agency (CFIA)** is the government body that regulates and monitors the organic sector.

---

[15] "Canadian Organic Standards and Regulations." Canadian Organic Growers, *Cog.ca*. http://www.cog.ca/about_organics/organic-standards-and-regulations/

Only "**Accredited certification bodies** are responsible for the organic certification of agricultural products and organic product packaging and labelling certification."[16]

Examples of accredited certification bodies in Canada are as follows:

Provinces/Countries	Accredited Certification Bodies
British Columbia	British Columbia Association for Regenerative Agriculture
Manitoba	Organic Producers Association of Manitoba Cooperative Incorporated
Nova Scotia	Atlantic Certified Organic Cooperative Limited
Ontario	Centre for Systems Integration
Quebec	Ecocert Canada
Saskatchewan	Pro-cert Organic Systems Limited
Italy	Consorzio per il Controllo dei Prodotti Biologici Società a responsabilità limitata
United States of America	International Certification Services Incorporated

For more information about the laws with respect to **food and agriculture regulations and Acts**, you may visit the website www.inspection.gc.ca.

MOVEMENT

"The growth and development of organic agriculture globally as an industrial sector, is led by

---

[16] "Part 1, Verification and Certification Bodies, Functions." Justice Laws Website, Laws-lois.justice.gc.ca. http://laws-lois.justice.gc.ca/eng/regulations/SOR-2009-176/page-2.html#h-4

many organizations that see its importance and economic potential. Whether organic farming is viewed as a way of living healthier ..."[17] by consuming food that enhances one's wellness, "... or it is regarded as a viable livelihood, it is being pushed to the point of being a worldwide concern.

Examples of these entities are as follows: in Jamaica – the Jamaica Organic Agriculture Movement (JOAM); in Nigeria – the Nigerian Organic Agriculture Network; and in Canada – the Canadian Organic Growers (COG)."[18]

The **Canadian Organic Growers (COG)** is a national charity organization founded in 1975 by Peter McQueen, who realized at the time that organic practices did a lot in protecting the environment.

Since then, COG has been the main driving force behind the advancement of organic agriculture across Canada. In an effort to have adequate representation across Canada, there are three (3) regions with local chapters. These are as follows:

Regions	**Local Chapters**
British Columbia	Island Natural Growers
	Vancouver Island
Manitoba	Organic Food Council of Manitoba
Ontario	Durham, Hamilton, Ottawa, Perth – Wellington – Waterloo and Toronto/GTA

COG is also affiliated with the following organizations:

    Atlantic Canadian Organic Regional Network (ACORN)

    Certified Organic Associations of British Columbia (COABC)

---

[17] Leroy Brown. (2012). Why Organic Farming is Great for Jamaica.

[18] Leroy Brown. (2012). Why Organic Farming is Great for Jamaica.

Ecological Farmers Association of Ontario (EFAO)

Saskatchewan Organic Directorate (SOD)

Internationally, COG is a member of the **International Federation of Organic Agriculture Movements (IFOAM)**.

IFOAM was created in 1972 "... in an effort to have an internationally unified, organized and more focused approach"[19] to growing and developing organic agriculture. "It has regional offices across the globe and is headquartered in Bonn, Germany.

IFOAM is accredited by the Food and Agriculture Organization (FAO) and the United Nations Environment Programme (UNEP). It is also recognized by the International Organization of Standardization (ISO) as an official standards setting body, and has observer status and privileges with the United Nations Conference on Trade and Development (UNCTAD).

Additionally, there are international organizations and events that are contributing to the global movement in different ways such as the International Society of Organic Agriculture Research (ISOFAR), the International Organic Accreditation Service (IOAS), and Biofach – the World Organic Trade Fair."[20]

---

[19] Leroy Brown. (2012). Why Organic Farming is Great for Jamaica.

[20] Leroy Brown. (2012). Why Organic Farming is Great for Jamaica.

Biofach courtesy of Tom Smith

INTERNATIONAL ORGANIC SECTOR

According to the book, *The World of Organic Agriculture 2012, Statistics and Emerging Trends 2012,* "… there are 37 million hectares of organic agricultural land (including in-conversion areas). The regions with the largest areas of organic agricultural land are Oceania (12.1 million hectares), Europe (10 million hectares), and Latin America (8.4 million hectares). The countries with the most organic agricultural land are Australia, Argentina, and the United States."

"About one third of the world's agricultural land (12.5 million hectares) and more than 80 percent of the producers are in developing countries and emerging markets."

Organic farming is being practised in at least 160 countries worldwide. There are 1.6 million[21] producers. Of this figure, India has the highest with 400,551,[22] followed by Uganda with 188,625,[23] and Mexico with 128,826.[24]

Globally, the organic market has grown by 288.8% since 1999 to US$59.1 billion[25] in 2010. "The countries with the largest markets were the …" United States (US$26.7 billion), Germany (US$8.4 billion) and France (US$4.7 billion), and the highest per capita consumption was in Switzerland (US$213), Denmark (US$198) and Luxemburg (US$177).

In 2010, there were 84[26] countries with organic regulations, and there were 549[27] certifiers in 2011.

---

[21] Research Institute of Organic Agriculture (FiBL) and International Federation of Organic Agriculture Movements (IFOAM). (2012). The World of Organic Agriculture, Statistics and Emerging Trends 2012. Rheinbreitbach, Germany: Medienhaus Plump.

[22] Research Institute of Organic Agriculture (FiBL) and International Federation of Organic Agriculture Movements (IFOAM). (2012). The World of Organic Agriculture, Statistics and Emerging Trends 2012. Rheinbreitbach, Germany: Medienhaus Plump.

[23] Research Institute of Organic Agriculture (FiBL) and International Federation of Organic Agriculture Movements (IFOAM). (2012). The World of Organic Agriculture, Statistics and Emerging Trends 2012. Rheinbreitbach, Germany: Medienhaus Plump.

[24] Research Institute of Organic Agriculture (FiBL) and International Federation of Organic Agriculture Movements (IFOAM). (2012). The World of Organic Agriculture, Statistics and Emerging Trends 2012. Rheinbreitbach, Germany: Medienhaus Plump.

[25] Research Institute of Organic Agriculture (FiBL) and International Federation of Organic Agriculture Movements (IFOAM). (2012). The World of Organic Agriculture, Statistics and Emerging Trends 2012. Rheinbreitbach, Germany: Medienhaus Plump.

[26] Research Institute of Organic Agriculture (FiBL) and International Federation of Organic Agriculture Movements (IFOAM). (2012). The World of Organic Agriculture, Statistics and Emerging Trends 2012. Rheinbreitbach, Germany: Medienhaus Plump.

[27] Research Institute of Organic Agriculture (FiBL) and International Federation of Organic Agriculture Movements (IFOAM). (2012). The World of Organic Agriculture, Statistics and Emerging Trends 2012. Rheinbreitbach, Germany; Medienhaus Plump.

AGRICULTURE CANADA

Agriculture and Agri-Food Canada (AAFC) is the federal government department responsible for the agricultural industry in Canada. "The activities of the Department range from the farmer to the consumer, from the farm to global markets, through all phases of producing, processing and marketing of farm, food and bio-based products. Agriculture is also a shared jurisdiction in Canada, and the Department works closely with provincial and territorial governments in the development and delivery of policies and programs.

The Department is also responsible for ensuring collaboration with its Portfolio Partners, which are also involved in regulating and supporting Canadian agriculture.

The Department includes the Canadian Pari-Mutuel Agency. This special operating agency regulates and supervises pari-mutuel betting on horse racing at racetracks across Canada."[28]

Its vision and its agricultural policy framework are as follows:

Vision

Driving innovation and ingenuity to build a world-leading agricultural and food economy for the benefit of all Canadians.

Agriculture Policy Framework

In Canada, agriculture policy is coordinated through a 5-year Federal/Provincial/Territorial initiative called Growing Forward. The **Growing Forward** framework agreement focuses on achieving results, reflects input from across the sector and delivers programs that are simple, effective and tailored to local needs.

The Growing Forward provides the following:

- Flexible programs that adapt to meet regional needs while achieving common national goals;

---

[28] "Our Responsibilities." Agriculture and Agri-Food Canada, Agr.gc.ca. http://www.agr.gc.ca/eng/about-us/what-we-do/?id=1360700688523

- Modernized regulatory processes and improved regulatory cooperation to support a competitive and innovative sector and for the betterment of all Canadians;
- And better service delivery through simple and accessible programs and services.

The AAFC has **partners** and **agencies** that assist it with its work. They are as follows:

Marketing Freedom for Grain Farmers

"*The Marketing Freedom for Grain Farmers Act*, which received Royal Assent on December 15, 2011, gives western Canadian grain producers the same freedom to market their crops as their counterparts across the country.

This changed to a voluntary CWB that brings new opportunities for producers, and innovation and value-added jobs to the Canadian economy.

Marketing freedom is about choice, the same kind of choice producers have had to sell canola, oats, and pulse crops. This is about prosperity and new potential for Canada's growing agricultural sector well into the future.

With the new law now in place, the Government is working with the CWB, farmers, our provincial partners and the entire supply chain, to provide information and support for the transition to an open, competitive wheat, durum and barley market in Western Canada."[29]

Portfolio Partners

Portfolio Partners	Functions
Canadian Dairy Commission	oversees pricing, policy co-ordination and marketing for the Canadian dairy sector.
Canadian Grain Commission	regulates Canada's grain handling industry and is also a scientific leader in grain quality research.

---

[29] "About Us." Agriculture and Agri-Food Canada, Agr.gc.ca. http://www4.agr.gc.ca/AAFC-AAC/display-afficher.do?id=1175599418927&lang=eng

Farm Credit Canada	delivers financial services to all sectors of agriculture: primary producers, value-added businesses and suppliers.
Farm Products Council of Canada	supervises the operations of national supply management agencies, and promotion and research agencies.
Canada Agricultural Review Tribunal	is a quasi-judicial tribunal that reviews Notices of Violation under certain agriculture and agri-food acts.

Canadian Pari-Mutuel Agency (CPMA)

The Canadian Pari-Mutuel Agency (CPMA) is a special operating agency within Agriculture and Agri-Food Canada that regulates and supervises pari-mutuel betting in Canada on horse races, thereby ensuring that pari-mutuel betting is conducted in a way that is fair to the public.

Federal Provincial Secretariat

The Federal Provincial Secretariat was established in 1988 by Federal and Provincial Deputy Ministers of Agriculture to serve the Federal Provincial Market Development Council (FPMDC), and the Federal Provincial Agricultural Trade Policy Committee (FPATPC).

In 1999, the Federal Provincial Agri-Food Inspection Committee (FPTAFIC) was also included within the Secretariat's mandate, and in April 2007 was dissolved.

Provincial and Territorial Partners

Provincial and Territorial Partners	Ministries/Departments
Alberta	Department of Agriculture & Rural Development
British Columbia	Ministry of Agriculture
Manitoba	Manitoba Agriculture, Food & Rural Initiatives
New Brunswick	Department of Agriculture, Aquaculture & Fisheries
Newfoundland & Labrador	Department of Fisheries & Aquaculture
	Department of Natural Resources
Northwest Territories	Department of Industry, Tourism & Investment
Nova Scotia	Department of Agriculture
	Department of Fisheries & Aquaculture
Nunavut	Department of Environment
Ontario	Ministry of Agriculture & Food
Prince Edward Island	Department of Agriculture & Forestry
Quebec	Ministry of Agriculture, Fisheries & Food
Saskatchewan	Ministry of Agriculture
Yukon	Department of Energy, Mines & Resources

30   AGRICULTURAL STATISTICS

Agricultural production is worth $130 billion[30] annually. Therefore, it is not a surprise that Canada is one of the world's largest producers and exporters.

(Contents on pages 30 to 33 and other parts of this book were originally published in ISSN 1708-4164 "An Overview of the Canadian Agriculture and Agri-Food System 2013." © Her Majesty the Queen in Right of Canada, represented by the Minister of Agriculture and Agri-Food (2013). Used by permission. www.agr.gc.ca)

In Canada, the agriculture and agri-food system encompasses several industries including the farm input and service supplier industries, primary agriculture, food and beverage processing, food distribution, retail, wholesale and foodservice industries.

The system provides 12.5% of jobs, employs 2.1 million people, and contributes 8% of total gross domestic product (GDP).

According to the report, *"An Overview of the Canadian Agriculture and Agri-Food System 2013"* by Agriculture and Agri-Food Canada, the agriculture and agri-food system is made up of the following:

<u>Consumers</u>

Changing consumer and societal demands are influencing the industry such as demanding more variety, more convenience, more environmentally friendly and healthier food choices, as well as food that addresses their values, e.g. organic and halal products, accompanied by proper assurances of quality and safety.

In 2011, Canadian consumers spent $181 billion on food, beverages and tobacco.

---

[30] "About Us." Agriculture and Agri-Food Canada, Agr.gc.ca. http://www4.agr.gc.ca/AAFC-AAC/display-afficher.do?id=1175599418927&lang=eng

Food and Beverage Processing

The food and beverage processing industry transforms primary production, and 34% of agricultural production was used as raw material inputs directly by the food processing industry.

Primary Agriculture

Primary agriculture is fundamental to the agriculture and agri-food system, even though it contributes just 1.7% to GDP.

As the number of farms decline, they are getting larger. It has been reported that there are 205,730 farms in Canada, down 10% from 2006, with the average farm size growing to 779 acres.

Total government (federal and provincial) support for the agriculture and agri-food sector was estimated to increase to $7.5 billion in 2011–2012, representing 26.7% of total agriculture GDP.

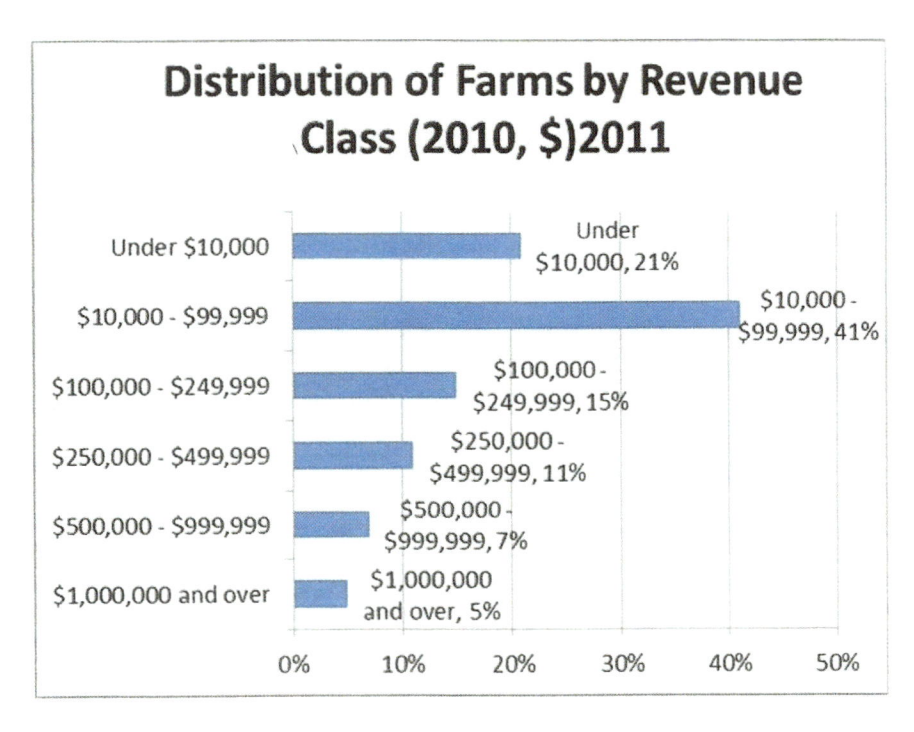

Distribution of Farms by Revenue Class (2010, $)2011

Revenue Class	Percentage
Under $10,000	21%
$10,000 - $99,999	41%
$100,000 - $249,999	15%
$250,000 - $499,999	11%
$500,000 - $999,999	7%
$1,000,000 and over	5%

Source: Statistics Canada, Census of Agriculture 2011

The top field crops by acreage in 2011 were canola, wheat (excl. durum), hay, barley, durum wheat, soybeans, oats, corn for grain, lentils, dry field peas and flaxseed.

The top fruits by acreage in 2011 were blueberries, apples, grapes, strawberries & raspberries, cranberries and peaches, pears and cherries.

The top vegetables by acreage in 2011 were sweet corn, green peas, carrots, green or wax beans, tomatoes, dry onions, cabbage, broccoli, lettuce and squash & zucchini.

The top livestock/animals by amount in 2011 were hogs, beef, cows, sheep & lambs, dairy cows and goats.

The top soil conservation practices in 2011 were:

- Crop rotation;
- Windbreaks and shelter belts;
- Rotational grazing;
- Nutrient Management Planning;
- Buffer zones;
- In-field winter grazing or feeding;
- Green manure crops for plough down;
- And winter cover crops.

The Canadian agriculture and agri-food systems (AAFS) which includes farm input and services providers, primary agriculture, food and beverage processing, food/retail wholesale and foodservice industries, accounted for 8.0% of total Canadian GDP in 2011 at $101 billion.

The AAFS is the third-largest contributor to national GDP after the finance sector and non-food manufacturing industries.

There were 293,930 farm operators in Canada in 2011.

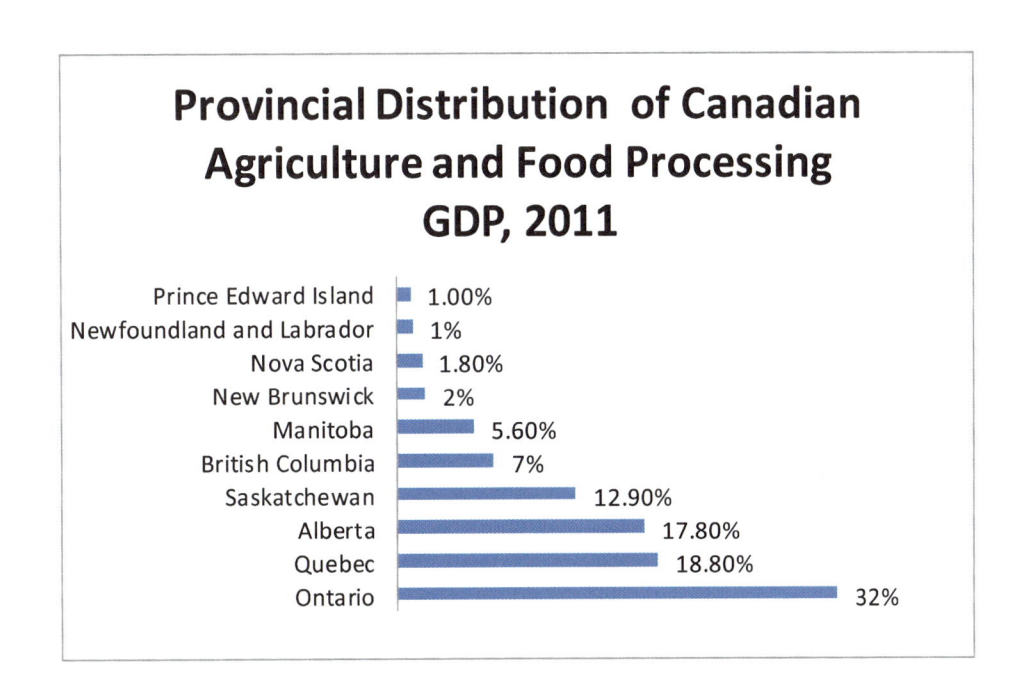

Provincial Distribution of Canadian Agriculture and Food Processing GDP, 2011

- Prince Edward Island: 1.00%
- Newfoundland and Labrador: 1%
- Nova Scotia: 1.80%
- New Brunswick: 2%
- Manitoba: 5.60%
- British Columbia: 7%
- Saskatchewan: 12.90%
- Alberta: 17.80%
- Quebec: 18.80%
- Ontario: 32%

Source: Statistics Canada and AAFC Calculations

Canada, with export sales of $40.3 billion, accounted for 3.3% of the total value of world agriculture and agri-food exports in 2011.

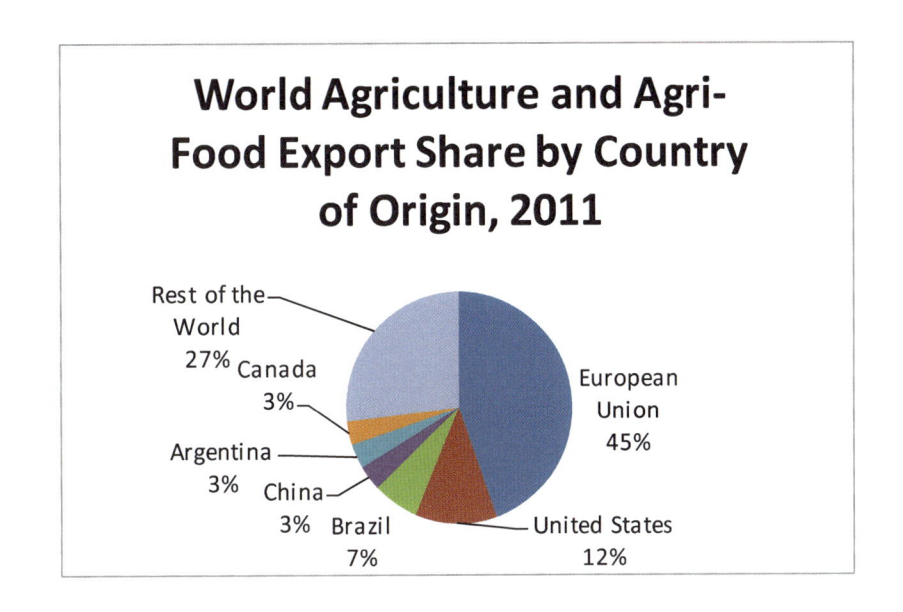

World Agriculture and Agri-Food Export Share by Country of Origin, 2011

- European Union: 45%
- Rest of the World: 27%
- United States: 12%
- Brazil: 7%
- Canada: 3%
- Argentina: 3%
- China: 3%

Source: Global Trade Atlas and AAFC Calculations

Leroy A. Brown   Why Organic Farming is Great for Canada

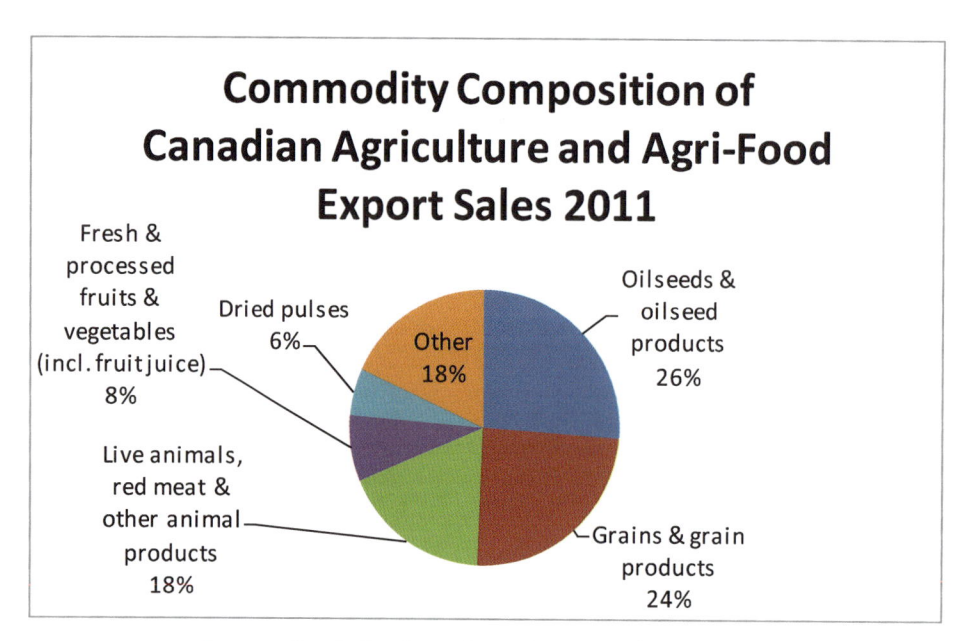

Commodity Composition of Canadian Agriculture and Agri-Food Export Sales 2011

- Fresh & processed fruits & vegetables (incl. fruit juice) 8%
- Dried pulses 6%
- Other 18%
- Oilseeds & oilseed products 26%
- Grains & grain products 24%
- Live animals, red meat & other animal products 18%

Source: Statistics Canada and AAFC Calculations

Canada had $31 billion in imports in 2011.

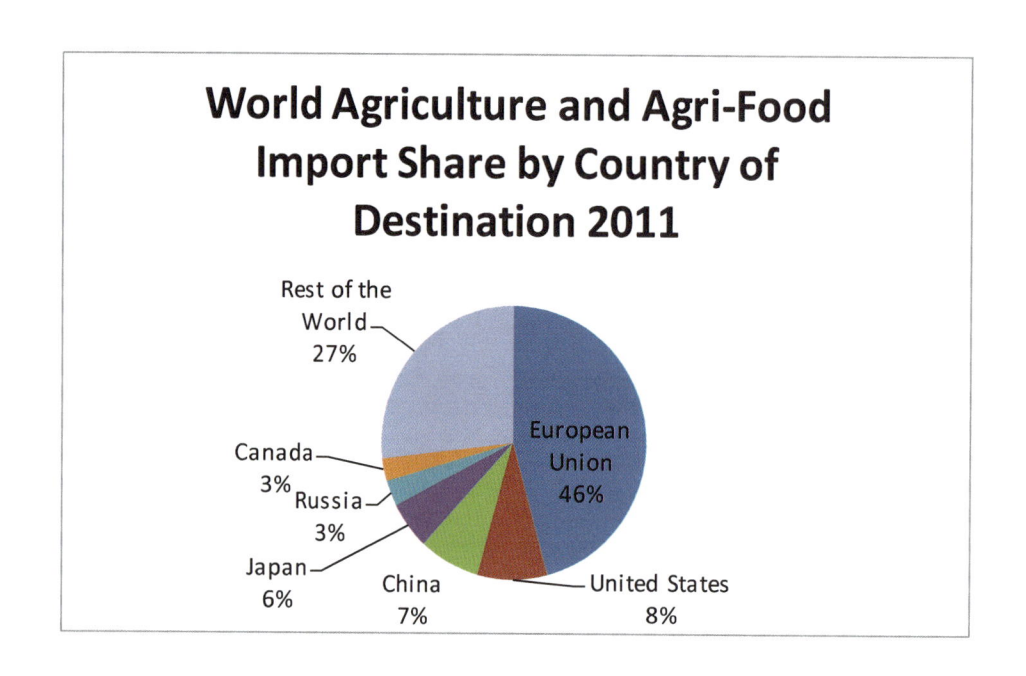

World Agriculture and Agri-Food Import Share by Country of Destination 2011

- Rest of the World 27%
- Canada 3%
- Russia 3%
- Japan 6%
- China 7%
- United States 8%
- European Union 46%

Source: Global Trade Atlas and AAFC Calculations

Leroy A. Brown   Why Organic Farming is Great for Canada

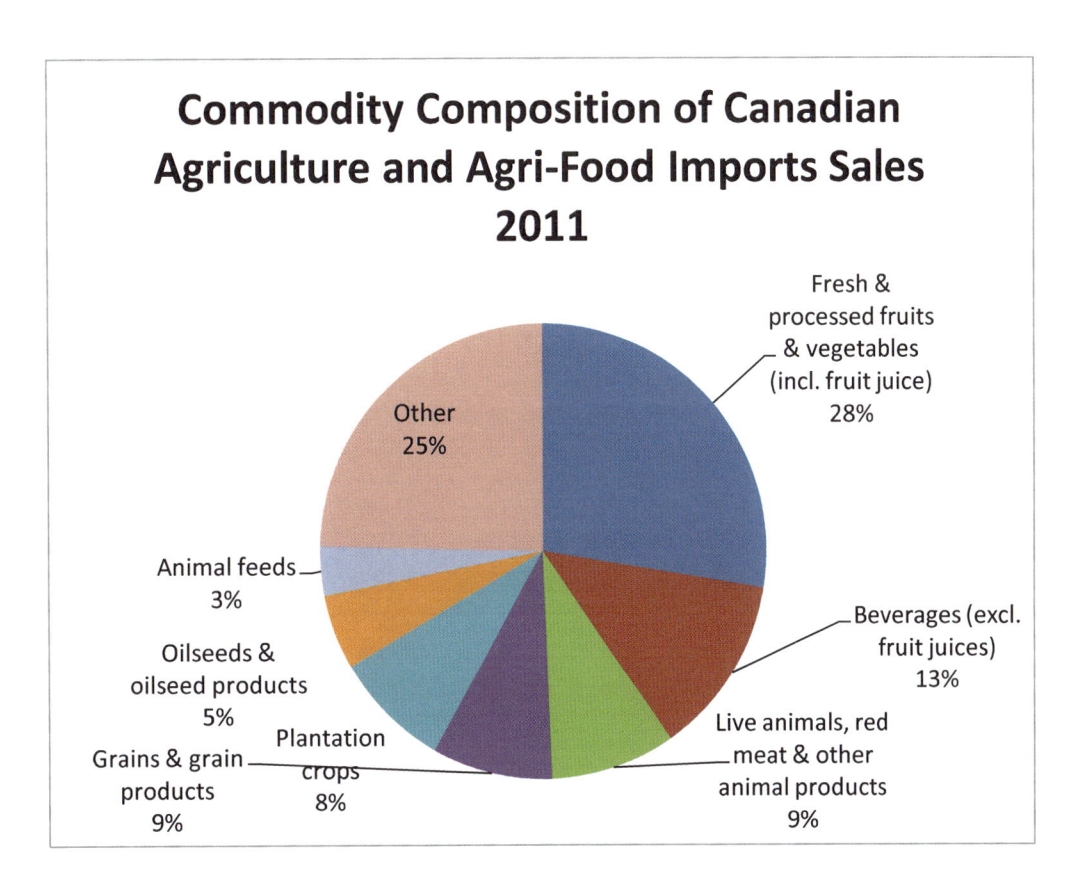

Commodity Composition of Canadian Agriculture and Agri-Food Imports Sales 2011

- Fresh & processed fruits & vegetables (incl. fruit juice) 28%
- Beverages (excl. fruit juices) 13%
- Live animals, red meat & other animal products 9%
- Plantation crops 8%
- Grains & grain products 9%
- Oilseeds & oilseed products 5%
- Animal feeds 3%
- Other 25%

Source: Statistics Canada and AAFC Calculations

In 2009, "close to 8% of farms …"[31] were young farmer enterprises (YFE).

Young farmers are identified as individuals between the ages of 18 and 39 years of age.

YFE refers to farmers 18 to 39 years of age.

---

[31] Agriculture and Agri-Food Canada. (2011). An Overview of the Canadian Agriculture and Agri-Food System. Ottawa, Canada: Agriculture and Agri-Food Canada.

Distribution of Farmers by Farm Group 2008

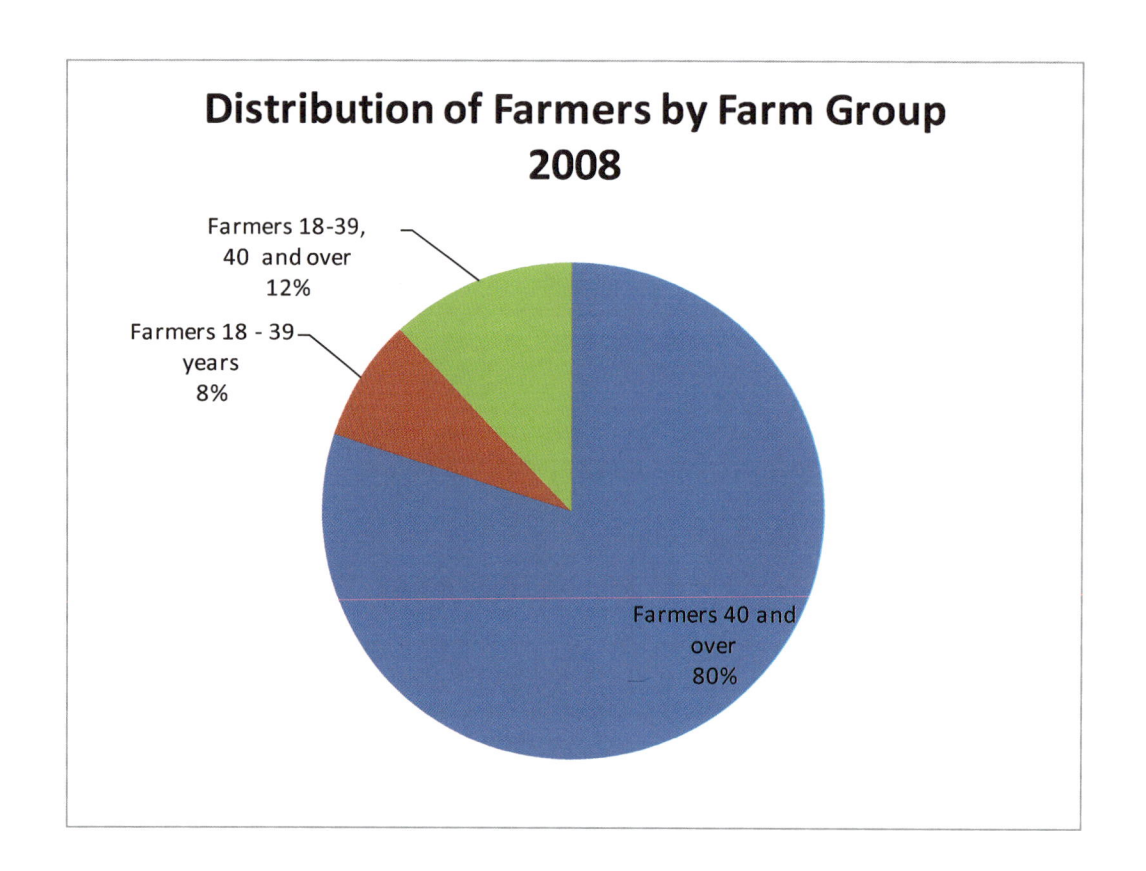

- Farmers 18-39, 40 and over 12%
- Farmers 18 - 39 years 8%
- Farmers 40 and over 80%

SOURCE: Statistics Canada, Farm Financial Survey, 2008 Reference Year

Leroy A. Brown   Why Organic Farming is Great for Canada

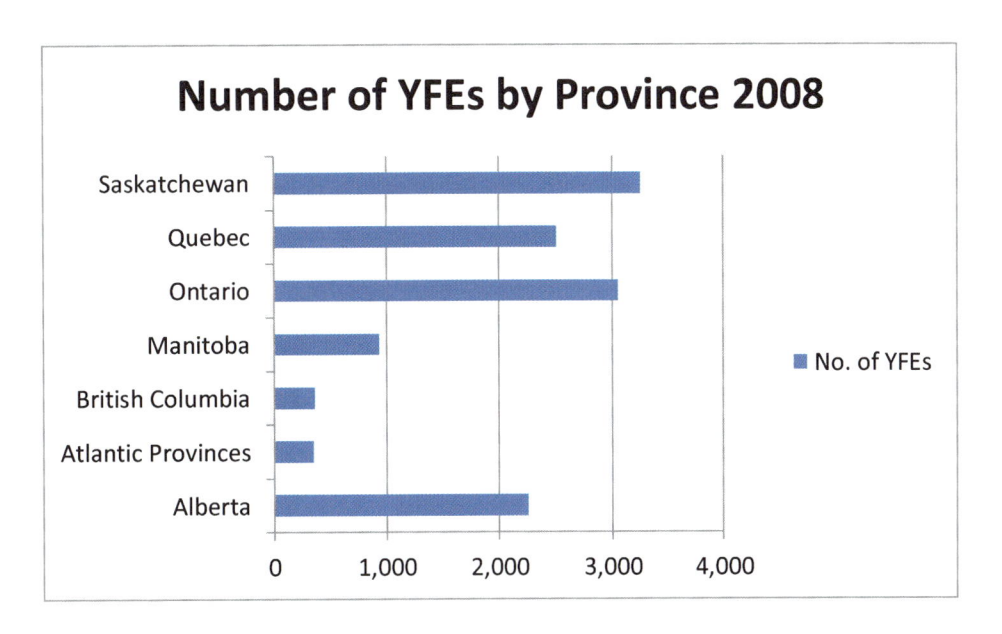

Number of YFEs by Province 2008

Province	No. of YFEs
Saskatchewan	~3,200
Quebec	~2,500
Ontario	~3,100
Manitoba	~900
British Columbia	~300
Atlantic Provinces	~300
Alberta	~2,300

SOURCE: Statistics Canada, Farm Financial Survey, 2008 Reference Year

In 2010, "YFEs accounted for 7.5% of Canadian farms ... but earned more from both farm and non-farm sources compared to older farm enterprises."[32]

Of all farm operators, about 48.3% were 55 years and over in 2011, compared to 40.7% in 2006; 8.2% were under 35 years of age in 2011, down from 19.9% in 1991.

CANADIAN ORGANIC SECTOR

"Certified organic operations represented 1.8% of all farms in Canada in 2011, up from 1.5% in 2006."[33]

In 2011, "... there were 3,713 certified organic operations ..., an increase of 4.4% from 2006."[34]

---

[32] Agriculture and Agri-Food Canada. (2013). An Overview of the Canadian Agriculture and Agri-Food System. Ottawa, Canada: Agriculture and Agri-Food Canada.

[33] Agriculture and Agri-Food Canada. (2013). An Overview of the Canadian Agriculture and Agri-Food System. Ottawa, Canada: Agriculture and Agri-Food Canada.

[34] Agriculture and Agri-Food Canada. (2013). An Overview of the Canadian Agriculture and Agri-Food System. Ottawa, Canada: Agriculture and Agri-Food Canada.

The top certified organic or transitional products by type of crops in 2011 were field crops, fruits & vegetables, animal products, maple products and herbs, spices or garlic products.

"Saskatchewan reported the highest number of certified organic operations in 2011 ..."[35]

"Canada's organic market grew to $3.7 billion in 2012, with national sales of certified organic food and non-alcoholic beverages reaching $3 billion. The value of the Canadian organic food market has tripled since 2006, far outpacing the growth rate of other agri-food sectors. A diverse consumer base is driving the sector, with 58% of all Canadians buying organic products every week."[36]

According to the report, *"Canada's Organic Market, National Highlights 2013"* by The Canada Organic Trade Association (COTA), organic food and beverage sales almost tripled in mainstream retail in the last six (6) years. Further information is as follows:

Sales Growth of Organic Products in Mainstream Retail ($ millions)

	2006	2012
TL Conventional Retail	586.3	1,350.3
Scanned grocery products	302.8	648.5
Organic fresh meat & produce	108.8	271.2
Retail channel adjustment	174.7	430.6

---

[35] Agriculture and Agri-Food Canada. (2013). An Overview of the Canadian Agriculture and Agri-Food System. Ottawa, Canada: Agriculture and Agri-Food Canada.

[36] "Canada's organic market now worth $3.7 billion - Growth driven by broad-scale support of organic foods." CNW, *Newswire.ca*. http://www.newswire.ca/en/story/1144253/canada-s-organic-market-now-worth-3-7-billion-growth-driven-by-broad-scale-support-of-organic-foods

Estimated Value of Total Canadian Organic Sales in 2012

	Sales Value ($ millions)	Market Share (%)
Total Organic Food and Beverage Sales (excl. alcohol)	2,978.6	1.7
Organic Alcohol	135.0	0.67
Organic Supplements	34.4	1.25
Organic Fibre (linen and clothing)	24.2	0.15
Organic Personal Care	41.1	0.45
Organic Pet Food	4.1	0.25
Organic Household Products	8.2	0.2
Organic Flowers	3.0	0.1
Organic Exports from Canada	458	
TOTAL CANADA ORGANIC MARKET:	$3,686.6M	

Canadian Organic Food and Beverage Sales in 2012

	Sales Value ($ millions)	Share of Total Organic Sales (%)
Mainstream Retail	1,350.3	45
Natural Health and Online Retail	864.7	29
Direct to Consumer	377.6	13
Foodservice/Institutional	371.0	12
Buying Clubs/Cooperatives	15.0	0.5

Leroy A. Brown   Why Organic Farming is Great for Canada

TOTAL CANADA ORGANIC FOOD SALES: $2,978.6M

Top 10 Categories with the Highest Number of Manufacturers Participating are as follows:
Tea – 29, Coffee (Roast & Ground) – 26, Juice & Drinks (Shelf Stable) – 26, Pasta (Dry) – 20, Hot Cereals – 17, Cooking Oils – 17, RTE Cereals – 15, Flour – 15, Bread (Commercial) – 15, Dried Beans – 13 and Rice – 13.

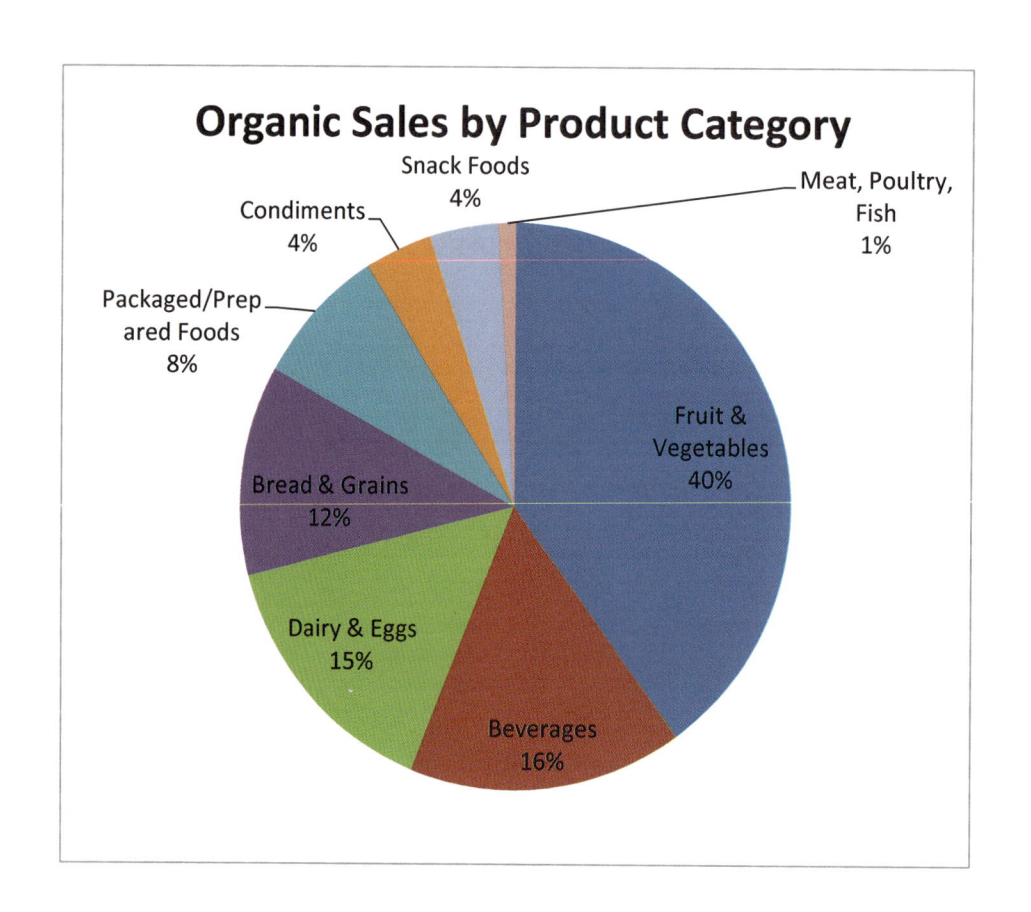

Organic Sales by Product Category

- Fruit & Vegetables 40%
- Beverages 16%
- Dairy & Eggs 15%
- Bread & Grains 12%
- Packaged/Prepared Foods 8%
- Condiments 4%
- Snack Foods 4%
- Meat, Poultry, Fish 1%

Top 10 Organic Pre-packaged Grocery category Segments

Categories	2008 Sales ($ millions)	2012 Sales ($ millions)
Soya Drinks	47.3	58.4
Milk	37.2	57.7

Leroy A. Brown   Why Organic Farming is Great for Canada

Coffee (Roast & Ground)	27.2	47.0
Yogurt Products	35.4	44.2
RTE Cereal	32.0	37.6
Soup	9.5	20.0
Eggs	5.7	21.6
Bread (Commercial)	3.0	19.0
Juices & Drinks (Shelf Stable)	9.8	6.0
Baby Food	1.4	2.8

Canadian organic products accounted for 43% by volume of organic food items that were researched (over 3,000).

The report states that 58% of all Canadians buy organic food weekly. It also articulates that over half of Canadians view organic farming as being better for the environment, and they

- **Consider organic foods a healthier, more nutritious choice;**
- **Believe ecological sustainability is an important consideration when choosing food products;**
- **And want to choose products that are not genetically engineered.**

SO WHY IS ORGANIC FARMING GREAT FOR CANADA?

THE OBVIOUS

- Canada has a large land mass and wide open spaces that can easily facilitate any farm operation.

- Canada has very suitable farm land, especially in southern Ontario.

- There are already established markets locally, nationally and internationally.

- Even though urbanization and industrialization are taking away suitable farm land at great speeds, there are still areas that are good for farming, e.g. Fraser Valley in British Columbia, Niagara Falls and Holland Marsh in Ontario, the parkland belts of Alberta and Saskatchewan, St. Lawrence River Valley in Quebec, Freshwater and Codroy Valleys in Newfoundland, and Red River Valley in Manitoba.

Parkland in Alberta courtesy of Cliff Wallis

Codroy Valley courtesy of Cornerbrook.net

River Meanders of the Red River, Manitoba

(Reproduced with the permission of Natural Resources Canada 2013, courtesy of the Geological Survey of Canada (Photo 2001-032D by Greg Brooks)

Leroy A. Brown   Why Organic Farming is Great for Canada

Holland Marsh courtesy of the Holland Marsh Growers' Association

THE ENVIRONMENT

- Because organic farmers are usually very resourceful and they exercise certain practices such as recycling, reusing, composting and saving seeds, they effectively contribute to cost and waste reduction.

- "Organic farms have higher soil organic carbon, which contributes to long-term yield stability and resilience in the face of unusual weather.

- Organic farms also appear to harbour more plant species than those in conventional systems, and they have a richness and abundance in birds and insect pollinators.

- Energy use is lower in organic agriculture. A study over 12 years in Manitoba, revealed that the use of energy was fifty percent (50%) lower for organic operations.

- Studies into various forms of farming have found that no-till and organic methods have the lowest global warming potential. These methods pull carbon out of the atmosphere and "sequester" it back into the soil.

- Because they avoid the use of fossil fuel-based fertilizers, organic farms also emit less nitrous oxide and other greenhouse gases."[37]

- "The practice of organic agriculture will help in soil erosion prevention.

- The practice of organic agriculture will help in restoring and maintaining soil fertility.

- The practice of organic farming will help to prevent pollution of rivers and other water ways, by eliminating or reducing pesticides and chemical run offs.

- The practice of organic agriculture will help to prevent potentially invasive species such as genetically modified (GM) crops.

- The practice of organic farming will help to conserve and protect biodiversity."[38]

DOMESTIC AND INTERNATIONAL MARKETS

- Because growing demand for organic food far outpaces supply, there is consistently an expanding market for organic groceries.

- "The biggest demand is for organic fruits and vegetables followed by organic beverages. The demand for organic grains and cereals are also strong. Organic beef is relatively low at one to two percent of total organic sales, however, it has the fastest growing demand of any sector."[39]

- "Organic food consumption is increasing everywhere, but organic production is not keeping pace. That means producers and processors are missing out on a profitable niche,

---

[37] The Globe and Mail. November 12, 2009.

[38] Brown, Leroy. (2012). Why Organic Farming is Great for Jamaica.

[39] McDonald, Ian. "Strong demand for organic food." Globalnews.ca. http://globalnews.ca/news/614660/strong-demand-for-organic-food/

and consumers are not getting as much local product as they could."[40]

- Domestically, organic sales are just about three per cent (3%) of agricultural production, which means there is a large untapped market for organic production.

- Canada is very dominant in grain production, which has assisted it in becoming one of the top food exporting countries in the world. Therefore, Canada is in a position to easily exploit its organic potential, and command a greater share of the domestic and international markets.

- "Organic agriculture, a worldwide growth industry, can be profitable, sustainable business for agricultural producers interested in going through the certification process necessary to enter this market. Organics have continued to expand during the last few years, and industry experts are forecasting steady growth of 9 percent or higher (OTA 2012)."

   (Reprinted from Organic Food Trends, Agricultural Marketing Resource Center, revised January 2013. Retrieved October 2013 from http://www.agmrc.org/markets_industries/food/organic-food-trends/)

- Canada's organic sales in 2012 is just about seven percent (7%) of global organic sales in 2010. From this, it can be assumed that in addition to its domestic market, there is a huge international organic market that can be ventured into more aggressively by Canadian organic food producers.

TOURISM

- With health tourism becoming popular, and with organic farming rising to its prominence partly because of health-conscious individuals, farmers have the opportunity to offer farm tours and visits from health-interested visitors.

---

[40] Roberts, Owen. "Organic Farmers Hunt for Cash Crop Farmers." *Organiccouncil.ca*. www.organiccouncil.ca/news/hunting-for-organic-farmers

- Because organic farming is environmentally friendly and does improve its surroundings, farmers can offer eco tours as an attraction to tourists.

- A "… fun activity that can generate good income is to have a pick-your own fruits and/or vegetable. This is where customers, tourists and individuals wanting a fun activity to do, can pay a fee and go on to the farm and pick their own food."[41]

- Organic farms can easily generate additional income from activities geared towards visitors such as site seeing, petting zoo, animal shows, etc.

Eco Farm Tour courtesy of http://roadstories.ca

HEALTH

- "… fruits and vegetables are valuable sources of nutrients that fight disease. They are naturally low in fat, cholesterol, calories and sodium; but rich in potassium, fibre, folic acid, beta-carotene and vitamins C and K. In fact, it is estimated that cancer rates would drop 20 percent if Canadians ate five to 10 servings of vegetables and fruit each day."[42]

---

[41] Brown, Leroy. (2012). Why Organic Farming is Great for Jamaica.

[42] "Brassica Family." Alive, Alive.com. http://www.alive.com/articles/view/16701/brassica_family

- Grass-fed animals produce leaner meat.

- Because conventional herbicides and pesticides are not used, organic food is less likely to cause dietary ailments and illnesses such as cancer.

- Organic food is known to taste better, and gives more substance – i.e. you taste more of the food.

- It has been found that some health concerns and diseases could be traced back to herbicides.

- "Organic offers that transparency and an audit trail so consumers know every ingredient in the process has met the organic standards, has been inspected and certified and can be tracked back to its origin."[43]

FARM OPERATION

- Approximately 35% of organic farm enterprises have revenues of $100,000 and over.

- "Capital input is relatively low as organic farmers are usually resourceful, i.e., they find other ways of doing things in a cheaper and better manner.

- Organic agriculture does not require a lot of tilling of the soil, so tractors may not be needed, thus immediately eliminating such huge expenses.

- The organic products sold are done at premium prices, so the farmer should be able to make a good living from his/her establishment.

- As the principles of organic farming are continuously followed, the farmer's inputs should be less and less, thus reducing overall costs. For example, less organic fertilizer may be required as more on-farm compost becomes available.

---

[43] http://globalnews.ca/news/614660/strong-demand-for-organic-food/

- Diversity is a core component of organic farming. So in doing this, the farmer is mitigating himself against financial risk. That is, with different crops being planted from different families, e.g., tomatoes (which is from the nightshade family and also includes potatoes, sweet and hot peppers), and peanuts (which is from the fabaceae family and also includes soybean, garden pea and alfalfa), if there is a disease outbreak in one crop, chances are it may not affect the other crop. Therefore, the farmer will still have produce to sell.

- Another financial risk that can be alleviated through the practice of organic agriculture is price volatility. This is done through crop diversification and crop rotation, as different crops planted together will command different prices. As such, if the price per unit for one crop falls, the shortfall may be accommodated for through the increase in price of another, or simply through the stability of that other crop's price."[44]

---

[44] Leroy Brown. Why Organic Farming is Great for Jamaica. 2012

EXAMPLES OF ENTERPRISES THAT SELL ORGANIC FOOD

BLACKS FAMILY FARM in MANITOBA

"The Black family's passion for producing certified organic milk stems from three generations of farming in Manitoba. Larry and Susan Black bought their first 320-acre farm in 1978, with just three milking cows. Today, the Black's 1100-acre farm is known as a staple in the Manitoba organic farming world. Creating and cultivating quality organic products has always been a family affair for the Blacks. Larry and Sue's two daughters grew up on the farm along with their one son. Recently their son and his wife became partners on the farm in 2005. The two are already training their one-year-old daughter in the dairy business, as she comes to watch the milking every morning.

With their dairy officially certified as organic in 2007, Sue and Larry were instrumental in developing MOM's (Manitoba Organic Milk Co-operative Ltd.). Larry is also an active board member of Dairy Farmers of Manitoba.

The Blacks feel privileged to provide organic milk to Manitoba consumers and are thrilled to be partners with Organic Meadow."[45]

Products: organic milk, wheat and alfalfa hay

---

[45] http://organicmeadow.com/who_we_are/our_organic_farmers/blacks_family_farm_larry_and_susan_black

CHOICES MARKETS in BRITISH COLUMBIA

"With seven stores and a rice bakery across Metro Vancouver and the Okanagan, BC, Choices Markets is Western Canada's largest grocer of natural and organic foods. From Kitsilano to Kelowna, our customers enjoy an extensive selection of organic, natural and local food items at fair prices. We're committed to upholding our vision while providing exceptional customer service in a friendly and welcoming environment. As proud locals, we'll always be 100% Canadian owned and operated, and fully committed to our local communities."[46]

"Since opening their first store in Vancouver's Kitsilano neighbourhood on December 6th, 1990, founding partners Wayne and Lloyd Lockhart have committed themselves to natural and organic food retailing. Fellow natural food enthusiast Salim Ahmed, joined Wayne and Lloyd as their business partner in 1998. Since then these three wise entrepreneurs have actively expanded the number of their retail outlets. In addition to … their Kitsilano flagship store, the three partners have added 6 sister stores (3 more in Vancouver, 1 in Burnaby, 1 in South Surrey and 1 in Kelowna) and a rice bakery specializing in wheat-alternative baked goods"[47].

Products: Bakery, e.g., breads and baguettes; Bulk, e.g., soup bases and snacks; Deli, e.g., low fat and organic cheeses and organic deli meats; Floral, e.g., bouquets and seedlings

---

[46] http://www.choicesmarket.com/default.aspx

[47] http://www.choicesmarket.com/about.aspx

Leroy A. Brown   Why Organic Farming is Great for Canada

FERME ALVA FARM in NEW BRUNSWICK

"With over 10 years of combined experience in organic agriculture, in Canada and abroad, Alain Rousselle & Eva P. Rehak graduated in agricultural technologies from the University of Guelph. They both gained experience CSA farming in southern Quebec, and started their own business in the spring of 2010 in southeastern New Brunswick. They want to supply superior quality vegetables and fruits to southeastern New Brunswick. **Alva Farm** supports sustainable agriculture, leaving a weak ecological imprint on our planet, while encouraging the next generation of farmers."[48]

Products

Ferme Alva Farm operates a CSA - Community Supported Agriculture which, is "… a concept which links consumers to local farms. Members buy a share of the produce at the beginning of the year and receive a box of food every week through the season. They can share the risks and rewards of farming and gain a better understanding of the real cost of their food, while knowing that they are investing in their local economy, culture, and food security. **CSA** also lets the growers focus on healthy, bountiful crops during the season as opposed to concentrating on mass production which reduces the quality of food."[49]

---

[48] http://news.fermealvafarm.com/index.php?option=com_content&view=article&id=47&Itemid=28

[49] http://news.fermealvafarm.com/index.php?option=com_content&view=article&id=46&Itemid=29

WHAT IS THE DIFFERENCE BETWEEN NATURAL AND ORGANIC?

According to the website http://www.stonyfield.com, the differences between natural and organic at a glance are as follows:

	Organic	Natural
Toxic persistent pesticides and herbicides	Not allowed	Allowed
GMOs (genetically modified organisms)	Not allowed	Allowed
Antibiotics	Not allowed	Allowed
Growth hormones	Not allowed	Allowed
Sludge and irradiation	Not allowed	Allowed
Animal welfare requirements	Yes	No
Lower levels of environmental pollution	Yes	Not necessarily
Audit trail from farm to table	Yes	No
Certification required, including inspections	Yes	No
Cows required to be on pasture for pasture season	Yes	No
Legal restrictions on allowable materials	Yes	No

Please note that in addition to the above, organic is regulated while natural may or may not be regulated. Also, organic has a specific definition, while natural may mean anything depending on the country, producer and/or culture.

For your information, xanthan gum is a popular emulsifier and thickener used in food and other things such as bread and salad dressings, toothpaste, etc., and is not considered organic.

INNOVATIONS AND HAPPENINGS IN CANADA

"Innovation is key to the agriculture and agri-food sector's productivity growth, competitiveness and sustainability."[50]

- There are organic conferences being held across Canada such as the Annual Guelph Organic Conference and Expo in Ontario; the Atlantic Canadian Organic Regional Network (ACORN) Organic Conference and Tradeshow in New Brunswick; the Canadian Organic Science Conference in Manitoba; and the Organic Connections and Trade Show in Saskatchewan.

Organic Connections and Trade Show courtesy of Organic Connections

---

[50] Agriculture and Agri-Food Canada. (2013). An Overview of the Canadian Agriculture and Agri-Food System. Ottawa, Canada: Agriculture and Agri-Food Canada.

- The Organic Science Cluster (OSC) has been created to drive scientific research in organic agriculture. It involves a network of scientists across Canada. All information is shared with stakeholders within the organic network.

- In 2008, Jessie Jollymore, a Dietician at the North End Community Health Centre, assisted in forming Hope Blooms. It is basically a social initiative geared towards affordable healthy eating.

  Hope Blooms is located in the inner city of North End, in Halifax, Nova Scotia. It is comprised of a community garden, a greenhouse, and value-added products such as herb salad dressing.

  The organization is operated by youth from the North End community, and they were successful in receiving $40,000 in funding from investors on Dragons' Den.

- The Organic Agriculture Centre of Canada (OACC) has been operating since 2001 to assist organic farmers and other stakeholders through science, education and research.

- Faculty members from universities across Canada are engaged in research related to organic farming such as Prof. Martin Entz, University of Manitoba; Mr. Bob Bors, University of Saskatchewan; Associate Prof. Dean Spaner, University of Alberta; Associate Prof. Martin Bunch, York University in Ontario; Assistant Prof. Valerie Gravel, McGill University in Quebec; and Prof. Alan Fredeen, Dalhousie University in Nova Scotia.

- There are also organic agriculture extension specialists and advisors across Canada such as Susan Smith at the British Columbia Ministry of Agriculture; Keri Sharpe at the Alberta Agriculture and Rural Development; Chantal Jacobs at the Saskatchewan Ministry of Agriculture; John Hollinger at the Manitoba Agriculture, Food and Rural Initiative; Evan Elford at the Ontario Ministry of Agriculture, Food and Rural Affairs; Danielle Brault at the MAPAQ – Centre de services – Granby in Quebec; and Susan Mackinnon at the Prince Edward Island Department of Agriculture and Forestry.

- The Growing Forward 2 (GF2) policy framework was officially launched on April 1, 2013, by the federal, provincial and territorial governments. It is a five (5) year initiative that is meant to make Canadian producers and processors more innovative, and in a position to take advantage of opportunities.

- The Government of the Northwest Territories, Fur, Agriculture and Fisheries Department intends to build on its Small Scale Foods Program. This and other activities

  will be done through the Canada – Northwest Territories (NWT) Growing Forward 2 Agreement.

  In an effort to guide and encourage those interested in participating, the *"Small Scale Foods Program, The Northern Lights Manual, NWT Small Scale Foods Program"* was developed. This handbook has been very useful for gardening in such arctic and sub-arctic conditions.

- Drones are being used in agriculture to determine where to water, and are also being used for land surveying among other things.

- The Agri-Innovation Program is a five-year program created to support innovation in agriculture by way of research and development.

- The Organic Federation of Canada (OFC) has been created to represent stakeholders of the Canadian organic farming sector. It also does other activities such as helping to create a list of acceptable agricultural inputs for organic products; being a part of reviewing the Canadian Organic Standards, and financing development projects across Canada.

- The Organic Value Chain Roundtable (OVCR) was launched in December 2006 to grow and strengthen the links in the organic sector.

- The Canadian General Standards Board (CGSB) is a federal government organization for standards development and assessment.

- The Organic Inputs (www.organicinputs.ca) website is a database that has been created to provide information to organic stakeholders about acceptable and approved items that can be part of organic operations.

- There are institutions offering organic farming programs such as the University of Guelph in Ontario and Dalhousie University in Nova Scotia.

- Canada has established organic equivalency agreements with the United States of America (USA), European Union (EU), Switzerland and other nations.

- In Manitoba, the Manitoba Agriculture, Food and Rural Initiatives (MAFRI) through the Canada-Manitoba Growing Forward Strategic Innovation Fund – Advancing Agri-Innovation Program funded the Green Garage project. This activity was designed, engineered and is owned by the Composites Innovation Centre (CIC). It was done to highlight a more environmentally friendly way in construction. So with the assistance of the Alternative Village at the University of Manitoba, CIC built a 16 x 24 foot single car garage, with some of the materials used coming from agricultural sources.

The Green Garage Project courtesy of the Composite Innovation Centre (CIC)

- The Canada Organic Office (COO) has the Operating Manual that contains policy and procedures. The COO also updates its website on Organic Products Regulations.

- SunOpta is Canada's largest distributor of organic, natural, specialty foods and natural health products. And it is also one of the world's largest organic ingredient suppliers.

- Crofter's Organic is considered the largest producer of organic jam in North America.

- The Canadian Biotechnology Action Network (cban) has been created to promote science and technology in such a way that it is better for the environment, ensures healthier food and so on.

- The Big Carrot is Ontario's first certified organic retailer, and offers certified organic dishes at its deli. It also has its Organic Juice Bar.

The Big Carrot Organic Juice Bar courtesy of DineHere

- In an effort to support entrepreneurs, innovators and world-class research, the Economic Action Plan 2012 proposes the following: $400 million to help increase private-sector investments in early stage risk capital, and to support the creation of large-scale venture capital funds led by the private sector; $12 million per year to make the Business-Led Networks of Centres of Excellence program permanent, and streamlining and improving the Scientific Research and Experimental Development tax incentive program, just to highlight a few.

- In an effort to improve conditions for business investment, the Economic Action Plan 2012 proposes system-wide legislative improvements to the review process for major economic projects to achieve the goal of "one project, one review" in a clearly defined time period for major economic projects, and $165 million over two (2) years for responsible resource development that creates jobs while protecting the environment.

- The Ontario Agri-Food Education Inc. has developed curriculum-linked agriculture and food-related resources, and offers profesisonal services to educators.

- Through federal, provincial and territorial funding, as well as funding from educational institutions and private sector, colleges have been able to use applied research to improve productivity for various entities. For example, the National Bee Diagnostic Centre (NBDC) is operated by Grande Prairie Regional College in Grande Prairie, Alberta, and it offers services to the Canadian beekeeping industry and research community.

- In an effort to make converting to organic easier in the dairy industry, Prof. Jim Fisher from the University of Guelph, personnel (which includes farmers) from Organic Meadows Inc., and Richard Broadwith from BCI Consulting, teamed up to make the 'Business Risk Workbook.' It is a "... risk management program to help milk producers determine if their farm can manage the transition to organic production."[51]

- Many entities are entering or expanding in the food business, such as Walmart Canada Corp. The company has launched its "... aggressive $450 million expansion this year snapping up former Zellers stores from Target, building up full food offerings in Walmart supercentres ..."[52] and so on.

- There is a thrust to provide locally and organically grown food through urban gardens. For example, Cultivate Toronto runs a community-supported agriculture (CSA) program across the City of Toronto using homeowners' backyards.

---

[51] Research Magazine. 2009 Agri-Food Yearbook Edition. Vol.XXIV, No.2, Summer 2009.

[52] The Globe and Mail. April 25, 2013.

Cultivate Toronto volunteers and interns preparing beds courtesy of Leroy A. Brown

AGRICULTURAL AWARDS

- In Alberta, there is the Alberta Century Farm and Ranch Award for "farm families who have continuously owned and actively operated the same land for a minimum of 100 years ..."[53]

- The 2012 recipients of the Alberta Century Farm and Ranch Award were Clarence and Helen Cyr and Sons. Their family has been ranching since 1910.

- The Ontario government has its Premier's Award for Agri-Food Innovation Excellence. This award includes:

    1. "45 Provincial Award winners with a cash prize of $5,000 each;

    2. 3 Leaders in Innovation Awards of $25,000 each;

---

[53] http://www1.agric.gov.ab.ca/general/progserv.nsf/all/pgmsrv51

3. The Minister's Award of $50,000 each;
4. The Premier's Award of $75,000."[54]

- For "… problem – solving ingenuity …,"[55] Victory Organic in St. Catherines, Ontario, received a Leaders in Innovation Award. This is because they (Bob Johnson and Vivek Rajakumar) created the Bob Wash. It is "… an affordable on-site answer to large commercial wash machines while at the same time providing the same degree of food safety."[56] Also, "it is able to handle a variety of vegetables, costs a fraction of industrial scale washing systems, and can be set up right on the farm. With Bob Wash, the product contains fewer insects and debris and has a longer shelf-life, which has increased the bottom line."[57]

Bob Wash courtesy of Jim Meyers and Ag Annex

- In British Columbia (B.C.), "The IAF Award of Excellence for Innovation in Agriculture and Agri-Food celebrates the innovative thinkers in the B.C. agriculture and agri-food industry that are responsible for generating economic, environmental or social benefits to British Columbia and the B.C. agriculture and agri-food industry. The award is open to

---

[54] http://www.omafra.gov.on.ca/english/premier_award/guidebook.htm#1

[55] http://www.agannex.com/energy/bob-wash-is-the-right-size-wash-unit-for-victory-organic

[56] http://www.agannex.com/energy/bob-wash-is-the-right-size-wash-unit-for-victory-organic

[57] Premier's Award for Agri-Food Innovation Excellence 2012.

individual producers, processors, agri-business owners/operators and other industry leaders."[58]

- An awardee of the IAF Award of Excellence for Innovation in Agriculture and Agri-Food is Dr. Timothy Durance. Dr. Durance is the 2012 recipient for the NutraREV technology. This technology is "... the first commercial-scale food dehydration technology, which is not only more energy efficient and less expensive than alternative methods, but also retains more nutrients. This promises to make a significant impact on B.C.'s agri-food sector, allowing producers of raw commodities to also supply value-added dry products."[59]

Dr. Tim Durance stands with the dehydrator at EnWave Corp courtesy of Brent Charleton

- Nationally, there is Canada's Outstanding Young Farmers Program. It "...is designed to recognize young farmers that exemplify excellence in their profession. Eligible nominees must be farm operators between the ages of 18 and 39 who derive a minimum of two-thirds of their income from their farm operations. Each year one farming couple is

---

[58] http://www.iafbc.ca/about_us/documents/12-01-26_AwardofExwinner.pdf

[59] http://www.iafbc.ca/about_us/documents/12-01-26_AwardofExwinner.pdf

selected from each of the program's seven Regional Recognition Events to represent their respective region at the National Recognition Event. At the National Event, the seven honourees are recognized for their achievements and judged by a distinguished panel of judges using the following criteria:

~ Progress made during their farming career

~ Maximum utilization of soil, water and energy conservation practices

~ Crop and livestock production history

~ Financial and management practices

~ Contributions to the well-being of the community, province and nation

Each year, two of the seven honourees are chosen by the judges as Canada's Outstanding Young Farmers.

The vitality of the Program is maintained by the continued participation of its alumni members, who return each year to the National Recognition Event to honour and welcome the new members. The OYF program is sponsored nationally by Agriculture and AgriFood Canada, Bayer CropScience, CIBC and John Deere Limited."[60]

- The national 2012 awardees for Canada's Outstanding Young Farmers are Sue Echlin and Vance Lester of Perdue, Saskatchewan, and Martin Brodeur Choquette and Johanne Cameron of St.-Charles-sur-Richelieu, Quebec. Sue and Vance operate the Living Sky Winery and Martin and Johanne are sheep and cash crop farmers.

---

[60] "About OYF." Canada's Outstanding Young Farmers' Program, *Oyfcanada.com* http://www.oyfcanada.com/about.aspx

L-R: Hon. George Webster, PEI Minister of Agriculture & Fisheries, Vance Lester & Susan Echlin, 2012 OYF National Winners, Hon. Pierre Lemieux, Parliamentary Secretary courtesy of Canada's Outstanding Young Farmers

L-R: Hon. George Webster, PEI Minister of Agriculture & Fisheries, Martin Brodeur Choquette & Johanne Cameron, 2012 OYF National Winners, Hon. Pierre Lemieux, Parliamentary Secretary courtesy of Canada's Outstanding Young Farmers

Leroy A. Brown Why Organic Farming is Great for Canada

65   IMMIGRATION

- In Manitoba, the Farm Strategic Recruitment Initiative (FSRI) was created through the Manitoba Provincial Nominee Program for Business (MPNP – B). It is geared towards individuals who would like to establish a farm operation in rural Manitoba.

INVESTMENTS IN ORGANIC AGRICULTURE IN CANADA

This is where some of the enterprises that have taken a more aggressive business approach to organic agriculture, and are actively striving to meet the demand for organic products and services in Canada, are highlighted.

ORGANIC MEADOW

Organic Meadow is a cooperative of mainly organic dairy farmers. It has a well-known organic brand and a variety of products, from organic milk and organic butter, to organic cream cheese and organic ice cream. Its products are sold across Canada.

It is recorded to have started in 1989 by a few farmers who wanted to meet the demand for organic dairy products. Also, these farmers wanted a structured and efficient way to get their products from the fields to customers.

So the OntarBio Organics Farmers' Cooperative Inc. was created and from then on, the Cooperative, the organic farmers and the Organic Meadow brand flourished.

M.O.M.

The Manitoba Organic Milk Cooperative Limited (M.O.M.) was started in 2006 by small dairy farmers in order to meet the demand for milk in Manitoba. Their collective milk is processed and sold under the Organic Meadow brand.

SUNOPTA

SunOpta is a worldwide company headquartered in Brampton, Ontario, that searches for, develops, and encases natural and organic goods. They are listed on the NASDAQ.

In 2012, their revenue was US$1.091 billion, and their gross profit was US$133.7 million.

ONFC

Ontario Natural Food Cooperative (ONFC) is among Canada's leading distributors of natural and organic goods. They started in 1976, and the cooperative distributes and supplies thousands of products. Its members are individuals who make at least part of their revenue from selling natural and organic products. It forms relationships with vendors who sell their products, and organize wholesale purchases through its Buying Club.

In 2013, ONFC bought the assets of Black River Juice Company. This purchase is intended to continue to achieve its mission, vision, goals and objectives, while expanding its network of goods.

GENETICALLY MODIFIED ORGANISMS (GMOs)

What is genetic modification (GM)?

"Genetic modification (GM) is recombinant DNA technology, also called genetic engineering or GE. With genetic engineering, scientists can change plants or animals at the molecular level by inserting genes or DNA segments from other organisms. Unlike conventional breeding and hybridization, the process of genetic engineering enables the direct transfer of genes between different species or kingdoms that would not breed in nature."[61]

So what is a genetically modified organism (GMO)?

It is a plant or an animal that has its hereditary material altered by way of genetic engineering.

Evidence-based examination of GMOs

According to the publication *"GMO Myths and Truths, An evidence-based examination of the claims made for the safety and efficacy of genetically modified crops, Version 1.1, June 2012"* by Michael Antoniou, Claire Robinson and John Fagan, "Based on the evidence presented in this report, there is no need to take risks with GM crops when effective, readily available, and sustainable solutions to the problems that GM technology is claimed to address already exist. Conventional plant breeding, in some cases helped by safe modern technologies like gene mapping and marker assisted selection, continues to outperform GM in producing high-yield, drought-tolerant, and pest – and disease – resistant crops that can meet our present and future food needs."

The publication, which is available at http://earthopensource.org/, went further to highlight the following:

---

[61] Canadian Biotechnology Action Network (cban).

- Myth: Genetic engineering is just an extension of natural breeding

    Truth: Genetic engineering is different from natural breeding and poses special risks

- Myth: GM foods are strictly regulated for safety

    Truth: GM food regulation in most countries varies from non-existent to weak

- Myth: GM foods are safe to eat

    Truth: Studies show that GM foods can be toxic or allergenic

- Myth: Roundup is a safe herbicide with low toxicity

    Truth: Roundup poses major health hazards

- Myth: GM crops increase yield potential

    Truth: GM crops do not increase yield potential – and in many cases decrease it

- Myth: GM will deliver climate-ready crops

    Truth: Conventional breeding outstrips GM in delivering climate-ready crops

- Myth: GM crops are needed to feed the world's growing population

    Truth: GM crops are irrelevant to feeding the world

Examples of Countries that have banned GMOs in one way or another

With help from the site http://naturalrevolution.org/list-of-countries-that-ban-gmo-crops-and-require-ge-food-labels/, countries that have banned GMOs in one way or another are as follows:

In the **United States of America**, Mendocino, Trinity and Marin Counties in California have banned GM crops.

In **Australia**, South Australia has banned GM crops.

In **Japan**, the Japanese people are very much against GM crops and seeds.

In **New Zealand**, no GM foods are grown.

In **Germany**, there is a ban on the cultivation or sale of GM maize.

In **Ireland**, there is a voluntary labelling system for foods containing GMOs.

In **Switzerland**, there is a ban on GM crops, GM animals and GM plants up to 2013.

Examples of Countries and Regions that approve, grow and/or produce GMOs

Canada

Canada grows GM corn, GM canola, GM soy and GM sugar beet. Canada also imports GM cotton seed oil, GM papayas, GM squash and milk products that contain bovine growth hormone.

The United States of America (USA)

The United States of America (USA) grows similar crops as Canada.

On Tuesday, March 26, 2013 *The Farmer Assurance Provision Rider* (otherwise called The Monsanto Protection Act) was signed into law. It expired by the end of 2013 as no extension was given.

Other Countries

Other countries that approve, grow and/or produce GMOs are China, Germany, Sweden, Czech Republic, Zambia, Spain, Slovakia, Portugal, Romania, Poland, The European Union (EU), South Africa, Britain, Thailand, India and countries in South America.

MY THOUGHTS

As is obvious by now, there is a lot more to organic agriculture than what one might have known. It encompasses more areas, and affects us in many ways.

Canada is in a unique and very good position, where it has an abundance of many things. It has an abundance of land, an abundance of water, and other natural resources such as trees. This country is one of the top exporters and importers of food globally. It has already established organic equivalency programs with other countries, and appears to have not been badly affected by the world recession.

Therefore, if organic farming was placed as one of the top priorities in Canada, then its economy should grow way above its current rate.

With approximately 35% of organic farm operations earning $100,000 and over in revenue, it demonstrates that it is a great way to make a living.

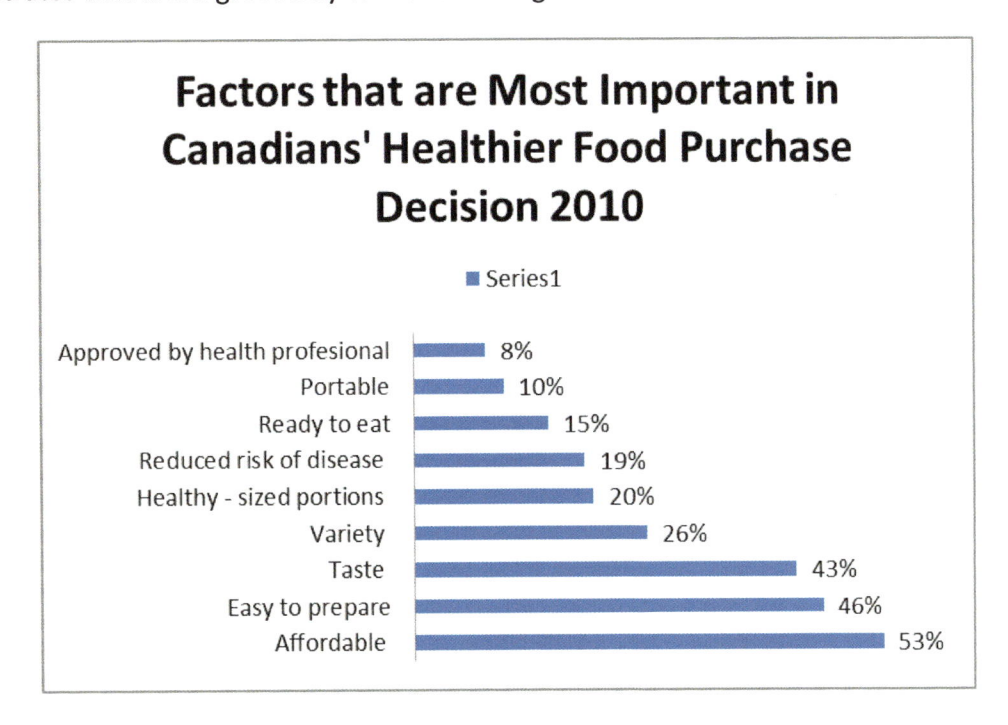

Factors that are Most Important in Canadians' Healthier Food Purchase Decision 2010

Factor	Percentage
Approved by health profesional	8%
Portable	10%
Ready to eat	15%
Reduced risk of disease	19%
Healthy - sized portions	20%
Variety	26%
Taste	43%
Easy to prepare	46%
Affordable	53%

Source: The Nielsen Company of Canada was commissioned by Alberta Agriculture and Rural Development to conduct this study in 2012.

Managing an organic enterprise is not easy, it is hard work! But if one can overcome the below-mentioned concerns, as well as others such as operational costs and weather patterns, then that individual will have a very profitable business.

The top obstacles faced by exporters of processed food outside of Canada are as follows: meeting cost required of customers, border security issues, foreign tariffs or trade barriers, distance to customers, uncertainty of international standards, meeting quality required of customers, and violation of patents or intellectual property rights.

With most of the suitable farming land being quickly developed into housing and other structures, acquiring land is getting increasingly difficult and expensive. Land prices have increased so much that owning property in Canada is becoming elusive.

As one progresses into the labelling of processed organic food such as organic yogurt and organic crackers, the following may be noteworthy:

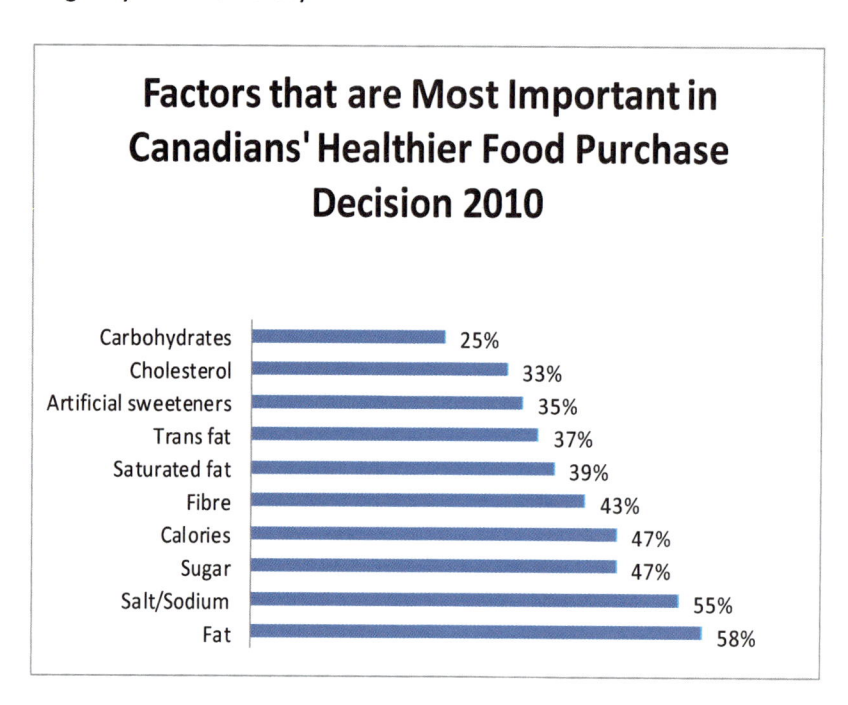

Factors that are Most Important in Canadians' Healthier Food Purchase Decision 2010

Factor	Percentage
Carbohydrates	25%
Cholesterol	33%
Artificial sweeteners	35%
Trans fat	37%
Saturated fat	39%
Fibre	43%
Calories	47%
Sugar	47%
Salt/Sodium	55%
Fat	58%

Source: The Nielsen Company of Canada was commissioned by Alberta Agriculture and Rural Development to conduct this study in 2012.

Among other factors, the increasing shortage of appropriate land on which to farm, and as food travels longer distances to get to consumers, food prices will continue to go up.

It appears that being able to consume food is not very important in Canada anymore, as most provinces have had a reduction in the acreage of farmland. By 2011, except for Nova Scotia, all other provinces in total have experienced an average decrease of 766,000 acres. It appears only Nova Scotia appreciates and values farmland, and by extension the activity of farming, as it registered an increase of approximately 24,000 acres.

As individuals worry about their health and where their food is coming from, in addition to the continued destruction of the environment, one should realize that organic agriculture is a natural solution for these concerns. Not only does it produce good, fresh and nutritional food, it is a guaranteed way of being able to trace the source of your food, as record keeping is an important part of this farming activity, in order to be certified organic. Also, the practices of putting back nutrient in the soil, the prevention of soil degradation, and the non-use of conventional chemicals, etc., directly helps to protect and conserve the surroundings.

Thus far, the top soil conservation practices in the overall agricultural industry based on 2011 information were as follows: crop rotation, windbreaks and shelter belts, rotational grazing, nutrient management planning, buffer zones, in-field winter grazing or feeding, green manure crops for plough down and winter cover crops.

This is encouraging, as it demonstrates care for the environment, and it would make it easier for conventional farms who are practising these measures to convert to organic, as they are already executing some of the principles of organic farming.

It is distinct that organic agriculture is one of, if not the only, economic activity that improves the health of living things, provides a good income for individuals, and has a positive effect on the environment.

Therefore, all concerns about having healthy food to eat, where one's food is coming from, having affordable nutritional food, and saving the environment, may be resolved in a simple way – support your organic farmer.

APPENDIX A

A Simple Guide to Starting an Organic Farm Operation

1. Note the difference: if you are doing farming because you simply love it, then it is a hobby. If you are doing agriculture because you want to make a living from it, then it a business.

2. Decide what you want to grow and/or rear, how much, who are your customers, where you want to conduct your operation, and if you have all that is required to make it happen such as financing, knowledge and labour force.

3. Whatever you don't have but will need, and you cannot use alternatives, devise a way or ways of how you can get it or them. For example, volunteer on an organic farm to learn organic agriculture, or prepare a business plan in order to submit to organizations for funding.

4. Get very familiar with the Organic Standards and especially as it relates to your crops, animals, manufacturing plant, retail outlet and so on.

5. Follow all requirements outlined in the Organic Standards, so you may become certified organic.

6. Make an official plan – do a business plan.

7. Register your organization with the respective body. For example, farm businesses in Ontario must be registered with Agricorp if they declare gross income of $7,000 or more under *The Farm Registration and Farm Organizations Funding Act, 1993*.

8. Becoming a member of a farm organization such as the Canada Organic Growers (COG) can be beneficial.

9. Get whatever permit or license that is required such as a Food Handler's Permit.

10. Keep track of the weather, so you will know when to start planting, or when the grass will grow in abundance for your animals such as goats, sheep and cows, among other things.

11. In the meanwhile, grow your seeds in a greenhouse so as soon as the weather is suitable for planting, you can start transplanting right away. Also, you may need to stock up on organic hay and other organic food for your animals, especially during winter months.

12. It is good to have refrigeration, cold storage or a cool area for keeping products such as organic tomatoes and organic beef.

13. Follow your business plan and change arrangements as is required.

14. Enjoy the wonderful life of organic farming.

Inside cold storage courtesy of Leroy A. Brown

APPENDIX B

A Simple Guide to Growing Organic Crops

With help from *The Gardener's A-Z Guide to Growing* by Tanya L. K. Denckla, the following steps can be taken:

1. Note the golden rule: if you take care of the environment, it will take care of all living things including you. Therefore, you should take very good care of the soil and its surroundings, and they will take care of the plants.

2. Earthworms, compost, mulch and living things like wasps are your allies. The earthworms help to aerate the soil and make castings that is nutritional for the plants. Compost provides nutrient to the plants. Mulch helps to keep water content around plants and keep down weeds. Some wasps prey on pests like aphids.

3. Know what is required for the particular crops you are going to plant and provide them.

4. Make a farm layout plan about where you want to grow each crop, how many, etc.

5. Make sure you are practicing the Organic Standards and doing activities such as crop rotation, intercropping, diversification and composting.

(Excerpted from **The Gardener's A-Z Guide to Growing Organic Food** *(c) Tanya L.K. Dencla. Used with permission of Storey Publishing)*

An example of what you may need to know about growing a particular crop

CROP: dried beans

TEMPERATURE: 60 to 75 degrees F

SOIL: ph 6.2 - 7.5

Does not require much fertilizing

Constant watering

Leroy A. Brown   Why Organic Farming is Great for Canada

SPACING:	2"-6" between plants
PESTS:	aphids and bean leaf beetle
DISEASES:	bacterial blight and bean mosaic
ALLIES:	Sorghum mulch
COMPANIONS:	beet and eggplant
INCOMPATIBLES:	garlic and onion

A simple way of irrigating plants courtesy of Leroy A. Brown

APPENDIX C

A Simple Guide to Rearing Organic Animals

1. Note the golden rule: if you take care of the environment, it will take care of all living things. Therefore, you should ensure the surroundings for your animals are clean and healthy.

2. Know what is required for the particular animals you are going to rear and provide them.

3. Make a farm layout of where animals will shade; where animal shelters will be located, etc.

4. Make sure you follow the Organic Standards and any other regulatory requirements.

5. Find out if your choice of animals is regulated by quota and abide by the rules.

6. Make sure you have enough land space.

7. Manage your grassland well.

8. Make sure you have proper housing for your animals if required.

9. Ensure you have adequate fencing, so your animals do not stray and get lost.

10. Have a veterinarian you can call in case of emergency.

11. Guard your animals from predators such as coyotes.

Organic Sheep being sheared courtesy of Leroy A. Brown

APPENDIX D

Example of Farm Layout

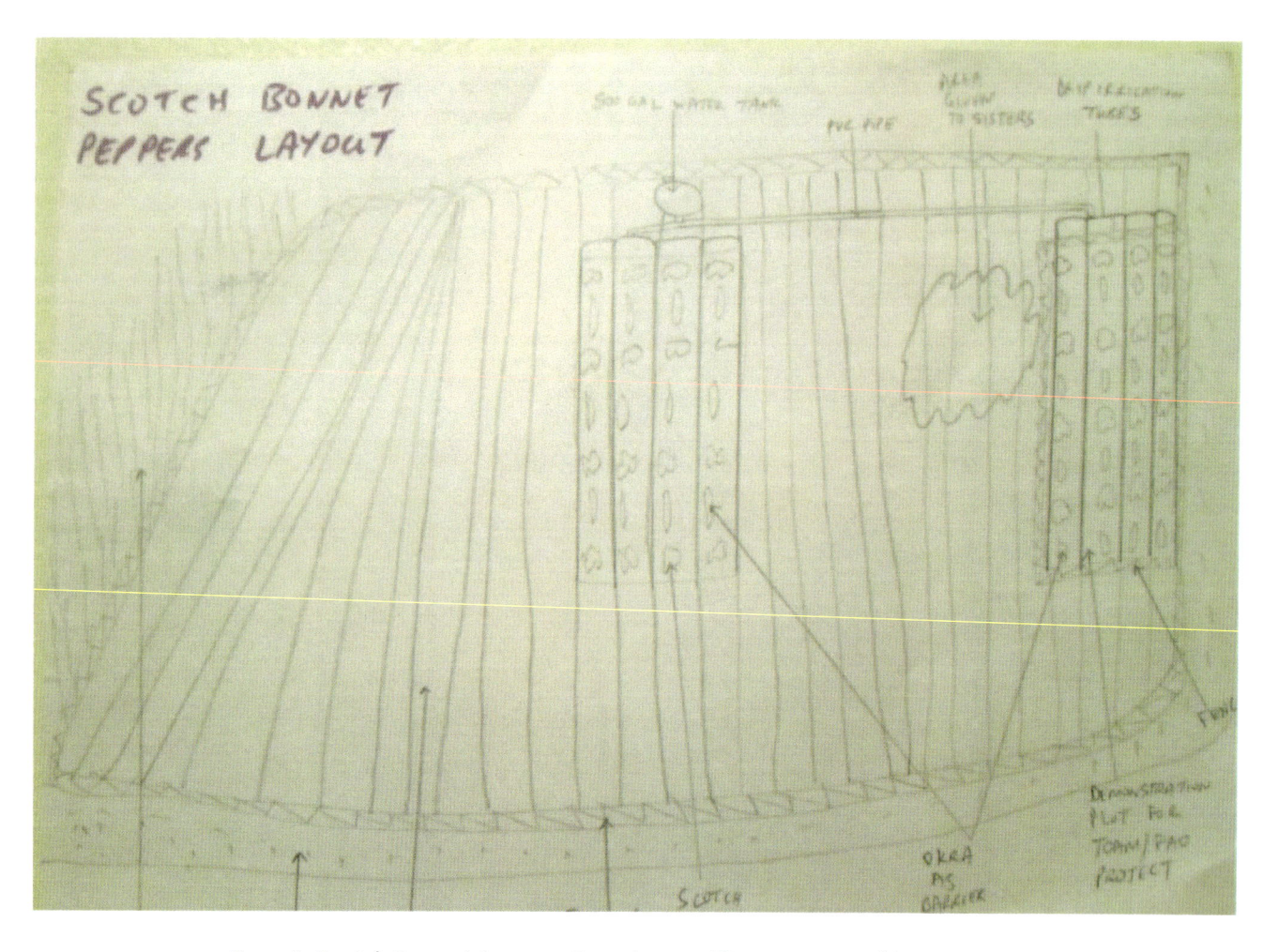

Organic Scotch Bonnet Peppers Farm Layout Plan courtesy of Leroy A. Brown

APPENDIX E

Components of a Simple Business Plan

A business plan is essentially a formal written way of expressing a commercial idea. The fundamentals of a simple business plan are as follows:

COVER PAGE – This page is the first and has the title and any other relevant information.

DESCRIPTION OF COMPANY – This is where you let the reader or potential investor/lender know more about the idea, the enterprise and its operation, who are the persons who make up the management, as well as the goods and/or services that will be offered.

MARKET ANALYSIS – This is where you outline how you plan to package, market, advertise and sell your goods and/or services. You also determine the customer you are seeking and who may be your competitors.

SWOT ANALYSIS – This is where you lay out your company's Strengths, Weaknesses, Opportunities and Threats.

FINANCIALS – This is where you show your projected cash flow statement, profit and loss statement, and revenue expectations usually for a 3-year period. You may also give ratios such as break-even analysis, company's efficiency ratio and inventory turnover.

APPENDIX F

Examples of Organizations in Canada Related to Organic and/or Sustainable Agriculture

NATIONAL

Agriculture and Agri-Food Canada (AAFC)

1341 Baseline Road,

Ottawa, Ontario K1A 0C5

Tel: (613)773-1000   Website: www.agr.gc.ca

- **Organic Value Chain Roundtable (OVCR)**   www.roundtable.agr.gc.ca

Canadian Food Inspection Agency (CFIA)

1400 Merivale Road,

Ottawa, Ontario K1A 0Y9

Tel: 1-800-442-2342   Website: www.inspection.gc.ca

- **Canada Organic Office (COO)**   (613)773-6222

Canadian General Standards Board (CGSB)

Place du Portage III, 6B1

11 Laurier St., Gatineau, Quebec, K1A 1G6

Tel: 1-800-665-2472   Website: http://www.tpsgc-pwgsc.gc.ca/ongc-cgsb/cn-cu-eng.html

Organic Federation of Canada (OFC)

12-4475, Grand Boulevard,

Montreal, Quebec H4B 2X7

Tel: (514)488-6192

Website: www.organicfederation.ca

- **Canada Organic Inputs Directory**   www.organicinputs.ca

Canadian Organic Growers (COG)

Suite 7519,

1145 Carling Avenue,

Ottawa, Ontario K1Z 7K4

Tel: (613)216-0741

Website: www.cog.ca

Canadian Biotechnology Action Network (cban)

Suite 206,

180 Metcalfe Street,

Ottawa, Ontario K2P 1P5

Tel: (613)241-2267

Website: www.cban.ca

PROVINCIAL

Organic Alberta

Unit #1, 10329-61 Avenue,

Edmonton, **Alberta** T6H 1K9

Tel: (587)521-2400

Website: organicalberta.org

Certified Organic Associations of British Columbia (COABC)

202 – 3002 32nd Avenue,

Vernon, **British Columbia** V1T 2L7

Tel: (250)260-4429

Website: www.certifiedorganic.bc.ca

Atlantic Canadian Organic Regional Network (ACORN)

- Includes **New Brunswick, Nova Scotia, Newfoundland & Labrador** and **Prince Edward Island**

131B Main Street

Sackville, **New Brunswick** E4L 4B2

Tel: 1-866-32-ACORN (2-2676)

Website: www.acornorganic.org

Organic Food Council of Manitoba (OFCM)

P.O. Box 68082 RPO Osborne Village,

Winnipeg, **Manitoba** R3L 2V9

Tel: (204)779-8546

Website: organicfoodcouncil.org

Yellowknife Community Garden Collective

P.O. Box 21,

Yellowknife, **Northwest Territories** X1A 2N1

Website: www.ykgardencollective.org

Nunavut Harvesters Association

P.O. Box 249,

Rankin Inlet, Nunavut X0C 0G0

Tel: (867)645-3170

Website: www.harvesters.nu.ca

Organic Council of Ontario (OCO)

5420 Highway 6 North

Orchard Park Centre – Unit 355

Guelph, Ontario N1H 6T2

Tel: (519)827-1221

Website: www.organiccouncil.ca

Act Respecting Reserved Designations and Added-Value Claims/The Conseil des Appellations reserves et des termes va lorisants (CARTV)

4.03 – 201 boul, Cremazie EST,

Montreal, Quebec H2M 1L2

Tel: (514)864-8999

Website: www.cartv.gouv.qc.ca/en

Saskatchewan Organic Directorate (SOD)

Box 32066, RPO Victoria Square,

Regina, Saskatchewan, S4N 7L2

Tel: (306)569-1418

Website: saskorganic.com

Growers of Organic Food Yukon

P.O. Box 20228

Whitehorse, Yukon Y1A 7A2

Tel: (867)633-4201

Website: organic.yukonfood.com

APPENDIX G

Examples of Institutions that Offer Organic, Sustainable and General Agriculture Education

Dalhousie University

Offers:	Various including Bachelor of Science (B.Sc.) and Masters of Science (M.Sc.) degrees
Example:	Certificate of Specialization in Organic Agriculture
Contact:	Halifax, **Nova Scotia**, Canada B3H 4R2
	Tel: (902)494-2211
Website:	www.dal.ca

University of Guelph

Offers:	Various including B.Sc., M.Sc. and Doctor of Philosophy (PhD)
Example:	B.Sc. (Agri) Organic Agriculture
Contact:	50 Stone Road East, Guelph, **Ontario**, Canada N1G 2W1
	Tel: (519)824-4120
Website:	www.uoguelph.ca

University of Alberta

Offers:	Various including B.Sc., M.Sc. and Doctor of Philosophy (PhD)
Example:	B.Sc. Agriculture, Sustainable Agricultural Systems (Major)
Contact:	116 St. Edmonton, **Alberta** T6G 2R3
	Tel: (780)492-3111 Website: www.ualberta.ca

McGill University

Offers:	Various including B.Sc., M.Sc. and Doctor of Philosophy (PhD)
Example:	B.Sc. (Ag.Env.Sc.) Agricultural and Environmental Sciences
Contact:	3415 McTavish St., McLennan Library Building, Montreal, **Quebec** H3A 0C8
	Tel: (514) 398-7878
Website:	www.mcgill.ca

University of Saskatchewan

Offers:	Various including B.Sc., M.Sc. and Doctor of Philosophy (PhD)
Example:	B.Sc. Agricultural Biology
Contact:	105 Administration Place, Saskatoon, **Saskatchewan** S7N 5A2
	Tel: (306)966-5788
Website:	www.usask.ca

University of Manitoba

Offers:	Various including B.Sc., M.Sc. and Doctor of Philosophy (PhD)
Example:	B.Sc. Agroecology
Contact:	424 University Centre, University of Manitoba, Winnipeg, **Manitoba** R3T 2N2
	Tel: (204)474-8808
Website:	www.umanitoba.ca

University of British Columbia

Offers:	Various including B.Sc., M.Sc. and Doctor of Philosophy (PhD)
Example:	Practicum in Sustainable Agriculture
Contact:	2329 West Mall, Vancouver, **British Columbia** V6T 1Z4
	Tel: (604)822-2211
Website:	www.ubc.ca

APPENDIX H

Organic Careers

As the organic sector continues to grow and develop worldwide, many careers have been and will be created, and will grow as demand increases. With help from the site http://organic.about.com/od/careersinorganics/tp/10-Top-Careers-In-The-Organic-Industry.htm, the following are some of the many organic careers:

Organic Farmer

This is the most important part of the organic food chain. This is where the quality of organic food begins. This is a skill-oriented profession, where an individual prepares the land, grows crops and/or rears animals, and return nutrients to the soil, among other things. This is done in such a way that the environment is protected; livestock and/or crops are certified organic; customers are satisfied with their goods; and the farm enterprise is profitable.

Organic Veterinarian, Plant Specialist and Technician

In these areas, trained individuals will be needed to ably assist organic farmers, organic handlers, etc. For example, if an animal is sick or there is a disease outbreak among the crops, then the solution to the problem given by the Organic Veterinarian or the Plant Specialist has to be made in such a way, that the animal or crops remain truly organic, and the farmer retains his or her organic certification.

Organic Certifier

As more companies and farms become certified organic, more accredited certifying agents will be needed. This person or organization ensures that the organic standards are being met before attestation is given that the goods, land, etc., are organic.

Organic Retailer

In this area, owners or operators of trade outlets such as supermarkets, grocery stores, specialty stores, and health stores can earn very good income from selling certified organic food and products, and especially at locations where people can easily shop.

Organic Agricultural Sciences Teacher – Postsecondary

According to Bloomberg BusinessWeek, organic and sustainable college programs are on the rise. As the demand for sustainable agriculture classes continue, the pool of schools is likely to widen more. This means teachers will be needed as well. Therefore, there will be demand for teachers trained in organic agriculture.

Organic Agricultural Manager

This is a person who is in charge of an organic farm operation, and ensures the day-to-day activities are conducted in a manner that makes the business efficient and profitable, while maintaining its certified organic condition.

Organic Chef

In this career, the individual will have the task of making exceptional food from quality organic products and ingredients, and being responsible for the overall function of the kitchen.

GLOSSARY

Advanced Technology – refers to a new technology that performs a new function or improves some function significantly better than commonly used applied sciences, e.g., biotechnology and nanotechnology.

Agriculture and Agri-Food Sector – is composed of all industries whose primary role is to produce food and agricultural products. It encompasses both primary agriculture and food and beverage processors.

Average Family Income – is derived by dividing the total family income by the number of families.

Canadian Agriculture and Agri-Food System – is a value chain of industries focused on producing agricultural and food products. It includes input and service providers, primary agriculture, food, beverage and tobacco processors, food retailers & wholesalers, and foodservice establishments.

Capital Cost Allowance – is the amount deducted for depreciable property for tax purposes.

Census Farm – is an agricultural operation that has the intention of producing at least one of the following products: crops (field crops, tree fruits and nuts, berries or grapes, vegetables, seed); livestock (cattle, pigs, sheep, horses, exotic birds, etc.), animal products (milk or cream, eggs, wool, fur, meat), or other agricultural products (greenhouse or nursery products, Christmas trees, mushrooms, sod, honey, maple syrup products).

Conservation Tillage – is the overturning of the soil to create a suitable environment for growing crops, and it is done in such a way that it conserves soil, water and energy. This is achieved by reducing the intensity of the tillage, and retaining plant residue among other things.

Crop Yield – is a measure of the amount of a crop harvested per unit of land area.

Direct Payments – includes the amounts paid under government agricultural programs and agricultural programs funded by the private sector. These are insurance programs funded totally by premiums paid by producers.

Farm Cash Receipts – include revenues from the sale of agricultural commodities, program payments from government agencies, and payments from private crop and livestock insurance programs.

Farm Net Worth – is measured as the total assets of the farm evaluated at current market value less total liabilities.

Food, Beverage and Tobacco Processing – includes companies that produce food that has been transformed in one way or another, e.g., apples are made into apple pies.

Gross Domestic Product (GDP) – is the total unduplicated value of goods and services produced in a country during a given period.

Gross Farm Receipts (GFR) – is the value of commodity production plus the direct transfers received by producers in the current year.

Hazard Analysis and Critical Control Points (HACCP) – is a process control system designed to identify and prevent microbial and other dangers in food production. It includes steps designed to prevent problems before they occur, and to correct deviations as soon as they are detected.

Incorporated Farm – is a farm that is a legal entity that is separate from the persons who own, manage or operate it.

Intermediate Inputs – are goods and services other than fixed assets that are derived elsewhere in the economy or are imported, and are used as inputs into the production process of an establishment. They may be transformed or used up by the production process. Land, labour, and capital are primary inputs and are not included among intermediate inputs.

Intra-Regional Trade – is trade between regions in the same location or zone, e.g., trade between Canadian provinces or the European Union member countries.

Labour Productivity – is a measure of an industry's output per hour of labour worked.

Market Receipts – refers to cash income from the sale of agricultural commodities, but excludes direct program payments to producers.

Multifactor Productivity – is considered a proxy for a country's innovation performance, encompassing technological change and other efficiencies. It tracks measures of labour, capital and land use.

Multi-Generational Farm – are farms with more than one operator, where the age difference between the oldest and youngest is 20 years or more.

Net Value-Added – is derived by calculating the total value of agricultural sector production, including program payments, and subtracting the related costs of production (expenses on inputs, business taxes and depreciation). Net value-added is distributed to the various factors of production, including rent to non-operator landlords, interest to lenders, wages and profits.

Non-Family Farm – are farms organized as cooperatives, communal operations, etc., and includes farms held in estates or trusts.

North American Industry Classification System (NAICS) – is a way of categorizing businesses based on their commercial activities.

No-tillage Farming – also known as **no-till** or **zero tillage,** is the practice of sowing crop(s) directly into the ground without the soil being overturned.

Partnership – is a commercial entity in which the business partners share with each other the profits or losses of the enterprise, and where there is no legal distinction between the owners and the business. All partners manage the entity, and are personally liable for its debts except in the case of a **limited partnership,** where certain partners may relinquish their ability to manage the business, in exchange for limited liability in the partnership's debts.

Primary Agriculture – is where natural resources are directly used such as land, to produce food, e.g., apples from planting an apple orchard, and beef, from rearing cattle.

Single Commodity Transfers – are transfers to agricultural producers from policy linked to the production of a single commodity, such that the producer must produce the designated commodity in order to receive the transfer.

Single Generation Farm – is a farm with more than one operator, where the age difference between the oldest and youngest is less than 20 years.

Sole Proprietorship – is a business owned and run by one individual, and there is no legal distinction between the owner and the enterprise.

Total Current Consumption – is the summation of expenses incurred for food, shelter, household operations, household furnishings and equipment, clothing, transportation, health care, personal care, recreation, reading materials, education, tobacco products, alcoholic beverages, games of chance, and miscellaneous items.

Total Factor Productivity (TFP) – is measured as output divided by all inputs (i.e., capital, labour, etc.).

WORKS CITED

"About." Ferme Alva Farm, *Fermealvafarm.com*. http://news.fermealvafarm.com/index.php?option=com_content&view=article&id=47&Itemid=28

"About Our Company." Choices Markets, *Choicesmarket.com*. http://www.choicesmarket.com/about.aspx

"About OYF." Canada's Outstanding Young Farmers' Program, *Oyfcanada.com* http://www.oyfcanada.com/about.aspx

"About Us." Agriculture and Agri-Food Canada, Agr.gc.ca. http://www4.agr.gc.ca/AAFC-AAC/display-afficher.do?id=1175599418927&lang=eng

Agriculture and Agri-Food Canada. (2013). An Overview of the Canadian Agriculture and Agri-Food System. Ottawa, Canada: Agriculture and Agri-Food Canada.

Agriculture and Agri-Food Canada. (2011). An Overview of the Canadian Agriculture and Agri-Food System. Ottawa, Canada: Agriculture and Agri-Food Canada.

"Alberta Century Farm and Ranch Award." Alberta Agriculture and Rural Development, *Agric.gov.ab.ca*. http://www1.agric.gov.ab.ca/general/progserv.nsf/all/pgmsrv51

"Always the Healthy Choice." Choices Markets, *Choicesmarket.com*. http://www.choicesmarket.com/default.aspx

Antoniou, M., Robinson, C. and Fagan, J. (2012). GMO Myths and Truths, An evidence-based examination of the claims made for the safety and efficacy of genetically modified crops. (Version 1.1). London, United Kingdom: Earth Open Source.

"Blacks Family Farm – Larry and Susan Black." Organic Meadow, *Organicmeadow.com*. http://organicmeadow.com/who_we_are/our_organic_farmers/blacks_family_farm_larry_and_susan_black

"Brassica Family." Alive, *Alive.com*. http://www.alive.com/articles/view/16701/brassica_family

Brown, Leroy. (2012). Why Organic Farming is Great for Jamaica.

"Business Immigration, Farm Strategic Recruitment Initiative." Manitoba Labour and Immigration, *Gov.mb.ca*. http://www.gov.mb.ca/ctt/invest/pnp-b/fsri/index.html

Canada Organic Trade Association. (2013). Canada's Organic Market, National Highlights, 2013.

"Canada's organic market now worth $3.7 billion - Growth driven by broad-scale support of organic foods." CNW, *Newswire.ca*. http://www.newswire.ca/en/story/1144253/canada-s-organic-market-now-worth-3-7-billion-growth-driven-by-broad-scale-support-of-organic-foods

"Canadian Organic Standards and Regulations." Canadian Organic Growers, *Cog.ca*. http://www.cog.ca/about_organics/organic-standards-and-regulations/

Chait, Jennifer. "10 Top Careers in the Organic Industry." *About.com*. http://organic.about.com/od/careersinorganics/tp/10-Top-Careers-In-The-Organic-Industry.htm

"CSA (What is CSA?)." Ferme Alva Farm, Fermealvafarm.com. http://news.fermealvafarm.com/index.php?option=com_content&view=article&id=46&Itemid=29

"Do 'Natural' and 'Organic' Mean the Same Thing? (The Short Answer: Nope)." Stonyfield Organic, *Stonyfield.com*. http://www.stonyfield.com/blog/natural-and-organic/

Engelen, Sarah Van. (2009, Summer). A smooth way to go organic. Research Magazine, 2009 Agri-Food Yearbook Edition. Vol.XXIV, No.2, p15.

"List of Countries That Ban GMO Crops and Require GE Food Labels." Natural Revolution, *Naturalrevolution.org*. http://naturalrevolution.org/list-of-countries-that-ban-gmo-crops-and-require-ge-food-labels/

McDonald, Ian. "Strong demand for organic food." *Globalnews.ca*. http://globalnews.ca/news/614660/strong-demand-for-organic-food/

Meyers, Jim. "Bob Wash is the right size wash unit for Victory Organic." *Agannex.com*. http://www.agannex.com/energy/bob-wash-is-the-right-size-wash-unit-for-victory-organic

Ontario Ministry of Agriculture and Food. (2012). Premier's Award for Agri-Food Innovation Excellence 2012.

"Organic Food Trends." Agricultural Marketing Resource Center, *Agmrc.org*. http://www.agmrc.org/markets__industries/food/organic-food-trends/

"Our Responsibilities." Agriculture and Agri-Food Canada, Agr.gc.ca. http://www.agr.gc.ca/eng/about-us/what-we-do/?id=1360700688523

"Part 1, Verification and Certification Bodies, Functions." Justice Laws Website, Laws-lois.justice.gc.ca. http://laws-lois.justice.gc.ca/eng/regulations/SOR-2009-176/page-2.html#h-4

"Premier's Award for Agri-Food Innovation Excellence – 2011 Program Guidebook." Ontario Ministry of Agriculture and Food, *Omafra.gov.on.ca*. http://www.omafra.gov.on.ca/english/premier_award/guidebook.htm#1

Research Institute of Organic Agriculture (FiBL) and International Federation of Organic Agriculture Movements (IFOAM). (2012). The World of Organic Agriculture, Statistics and Emerging Trends 2012. Rheinbreitbach, Germany: Medienhaus Plump.

Roberts, Owen. "Organic Farmers Hunt for Cash Crop Farmers." *Organiccouncil.ca*. www.organiccouncil.ca/news/hunting-for-organic-farmers

"Significance of the Food and Beverage Processing Industry in Canada." Agriculture and Agri-Food Canada, *Agr.gc.ca*. http://www.agr.gc.ca/eng/industry-markets-and-trade/statistics-and-market-information/by-product-sector/processed-food-and-beverages/significance-of-the-food-and-beverage-processing-industry-in-canada/?id=1174563085690

The Globe and Mail. April 25, 2013

The Globe and Mail. November 12, 2009

"Vancouver Entrepreneur Wins Award of Excellence for Innovation." Investment Agriculture Foundation of British Columbia, *Iafbc.ca*. http://www.iafbc.ca/about_us/documents/12-01-26_AwardofExwinner.pdf

"What is organic?" Canadian Organic Growers, *Cog.ca*. http://www.cog.ca/about_organics/what_is_organics/

INDEX

A

Accredited certification bodies 21

Acts 21

Agriculture & Agri-Food Canada 26, 30

Agriculture Policy Framework 26

Agri-food 15, 30, 31-35

Annual Guelph Organic Conference & Expo 54

Atlantic Canadian Organic Regional Network (ACORN) 22, 54

B

Biodiversity 45

Biofach 23-24

C

Canada 10, 14-17

Canada Act 14

Canada Agricultural Review Tribunal 28

Canadian Dairy Commission 27

Canadian Food Inspection Agency 20

Canadian Grain Commission 27

Canadian Organic Growers (COG) 18, 22-23

Canadian Organic Science Conference 52

Canadian Pari-Mutuel Agency 26, 28

Canadian Shield 13-14

Certifier 18

Codroy Valley 42-43

Constitution Act 14

D

Denmark 11, 25

E

Ecological 10, 19

E-commerce 10

Economic Action Plan 2012 58

Environmentally 11, 15, 47

Europe 24

F

Farm Credit Canada 28

Farm Products Council of Canada 28

Farm Strategic Recruitment Initiative (FSRI) 65

Federal 26, 28

First Nations 14

Food 10, 18, 22, 45

Food and Agriculture Organization (FAO) 23

Food & Beverage 16-17, 29, 37

France 11

Fraser Valley 40

Freshwater Valley 40

Functional Foods 16

G

Genetically modified 18, 68

Germany 11, 23, 25

Globally 10, 15

Global Warming 45

Greenpeace 15

Gross Domestic Product (GDP) 30-33

Growing Forward 26, 55

H

Healthier 10, 18, 22

Holland Marsh 42-43

Hope Blooms 55

I

India 25

International Organic Accreditation Service (IOAS) 23

International Organization of Standardization (ISO) 23

International Society of Organic Agriculture Research (ISOFAR) 23

Inuit 14

J

Jamaica Organic Agriculture Movement (JOAM) 22

K

Keri Sharpe 55

L

Land 15, 24

Larger farm 10

Latin America 24

Livestock 19

Luxemburg 11, 25

M

Mainstream 10

Marketing Freedom for Grain Farmers Act 27

Mexico 25

N

Natural 53

Niagara Falls 42

Nigerian Organic Agriculture Network 22

North America 12-14

O

Oceania 23

Organic 18-22, 25, 37-41, 45-53, 55, 57-58, 66, 67

Organic Connections & Trade Show 54

Organic Equivalency Agreements 57

Organic Farming 10, 22, 25, 45

Organic Monitor 11

Ottawa 15

P

Parkland belts 42

Peter McQueen 22

Portfolio Partners 27

Q

Quasi-judicial 28

R

Recycling 44

Red River Valley 42-43

Regulations 21

Retail outlets 10

S

Scotiabank Caribbean Carnival 13

St. Lawrence River Valley 42

Sustainable 10

Switzerland 11, 25

T

Tribunal 28

U

Uganda 25

United Nations Conference on Trade & Development (UNCTAD) 23

United Nations Environment Programme (UNEP) 23

United States 11, 25

Urbanization 42

V

Violation 28

W

War of 1812 14

World Organic Trade Fair 23

Worldwide 10, 22

X

Xanthan gum 53

Y

Young farmer 35

Z

Zoo 47

Made in the USA
Charleston, SC
19 September 2014